Walking With Prophets and Kings

by Steven J. Wallace

© 2020 One Stone Press.
All rights reserved. No part of this book may be reproduced in any form without written permission of the publisher.

Published by:
One Stone Press
979 Lovers Lane
Bowling Green, KY 42103

Printed in the United States of America

ISBN: 978-1-941422-56-4

www.onestone.com

Table of Contents

LESSON 1 Walking With Samuel: The Last Judge 5

LESSON 2 Walking With Saul: A King Like the Nations 13

LESSON 3 Walking With David: A King After God's Own Heart 21

LESSON 4 Walking With Solomon: A King Who Had It All 29

LESSON 5 Walking With Rehoboam and Jeroboam: A Kingdom Divides 37

LESSON 6 Walking With Jehoshaphat: The Danger of Evil Companionship 45

LESSON 7 Walking With Elijah: The Challenger of False Religion 53

LESSON 8 Walking With Elisha: Possessing a Double Spirit 61

LESSON 9 Walking With King Jehu: Unfaithful Zeal 69

LESSON 10 Walking With King Hezekiah: Strengthened by God 75

LESSON 11 Walking Into the Collapse and Fall of a Kingdom 83

LESSON 12 Walking With Ezra to Rebuild the Law in Israel 91

LESSON 13 Walking With Nehemiah to Rebuild the Walls of Jerusalem 97

Dedication

I dedicate this work to my loving wife, Kelly, who has tirelessly supported me in doing the work of an evangelist. I also dedicate this work to my three children, Nick, Ethan, and Danielle, who are the joy of my fatherhood. Without their individual input and keen insight, this material would have suffered and would not have taken the form it now has.

Lesson 1

Walking With Samuel: The Last Judge

Introduction to the Life of Samuel (1 Samuel 1:1-2:21)

I was born around 1100 BC to God-fearing parents Elkanah and Hannah. I was named Samuel, which means "heard by God," because God heard my mother's prayerful cries. See, my mother was barren—until one day when the Lord answered her prayer. She offered it before the tabernacle, where she poured out her soul before Him (1 Samuel 1:9-18). God answered her prayer and took away her reproach by giving her a son. My mother dedicated me to the priesthood, where even as a child I ministered to the Lord, working with Eli (1 Samuel 2:11; 3:1). Sadly, even those who served as priests were wicked (1 Samuel 2:12).

In addition to being a priest, I was also a prophet; God spoke through me. I was a boy the first time I heard Him speak and thought it was my mentor, Eli, calling me (1 Samuel 3:4-8). I had to tell people what God wanted, even when it was not pleasant or easy. My first message from God was very hard, for it was against the house of Eli. I was afraid to tell him (1 Samuel 3:15). Eli helped me learn then that I cannot hide anything that God has revealed, even when it is most unpleasant, so I told him everything (1 Samuel 3:16-18). The words God gave me proved true every time; they did not "fall to the ground" (1 Samuel 3:19).

I also became the last judge of the nation of Israel, ending the dark period of the judges. In that period, my countrymen had become very corrupt and idolatrous. They lived their lives however they thought was right, rather than what God thought (Judges 21:25). As a result, my country was poor

> **KEY PASSAGE**
>
> After that He gave them **judges** for about four hundred and fifty years, until **Samuel the prophet**.
>
> - Acts 13:20

FUN FACTS ABOUT SAMUEL

- Born from the barren
- Served the Lord as a little boy
- Has two books named after him, but he doesn't appear in the second
- The last judge of Israel
- Anointed the first two kings of Israel
- Spoke to the living after he died

and war-torn. We often became subject to the violence of neighboring countries. At times we were overrun with enemies and had to seek shelter in the mountains, living in caves, dens, and even thickets and pits (Judges 6:2; 1 Samuel 13:6)! Life was hard then. The Philistines were a dominant threat to our survival. I would eventually anoint the first two kings of Israel. The first, Saul, became a great disappointment. The second king, David, became a mighty warrior-king who liberated us from our enemies. My name is Samuel. *Come walk with me in my history.*

Samuel's life and walk are remarkable. He is mentioned by other Bible writers and is with the company of those mentioned as heroes of faith in Hebrews 11:32. Jeremiah the prophet connects him with Moses, where he is noted as a persuasive person. God said, "Even if Moses and Samuel stood before Me, My mind would not be favorable toward this people" (Jeremiah 15:1).

During the early days of Samuel's life, the tribes of Israel had no centralized government; they had no earthly king reigning over them or fighting their battles. God alone was their king. They were independent of each other but could achieve unity. They did this through dependence on and faithfulness to the Lord and the Covenant given by Moses. Local churches of Christ function in much of the same way today. No church rules over another church. Jesus is our king. Unity among us is derived from our devotion and obedience to Jesus and His Covenant.

The adversaries to Israel (1 Samuel 2:22-6:19)

1. A WICKED AND TOLERANT PRIESTHOOD

Eli, the current judge and a priest, had very wicked sons serving in the priesthood (1 Samuel 2:12-17, 22). Because of their vile behavior, God was going to judge Eli's house and remove his sons from serving as priests (1 Samuel 3:13-14). They despised the offering of the Lord (1 Samuel 2:17).

Fill in the blanks

1 Samuel 3:12-13:
"In that day I will perform against Eli all that I have spoken concerning his _____, from beginning to end. For I have told him that I will judge his _____ forever for the iniquity which he knows, because his _____ made themselves _____, and he did not _____ them."

Questions

1. Why was Samuel afraid to tell the word of the Lord to Eli? _____

2. What must a faithful evangelist preach even when the message may not be welcomed to some of the listeners in the church (2 Timothy 4:1-4)?

3. How has the Lord revealed His will to us today (Ephesians 3:3-5)? _____

4. What house was God going to judge (1 Samuel 3:12-14)? Was this a dwelling place or a household? _____

5. Although Eli asked his sons about their evil dealings with the people and spoke against what they did (1 Samuel 2:22-24), he nonetheless "did not restrain them" (3:13). Explain what this means. What else do you suppose Eli should have done? _____

6. Have you considered how your actions affect your father's house in a positive or negative way? What ways can negatively affect your father's house? How can you have a positive effect? _____

7. How might your actions affect God's house—the church? What kind of effect would an example of lying, cheating, stealing, cursing, dressing immodestly, or sexual immorality have? What kind of effect would humility, respect for elders, active participation in worship and Bible study, and the general fear of the Lord have? _____

_____
_____
_____
_____

8. Read Malachi 2:5-7 and describe what kind of people priests were to be like. _____

_____
_____

2. THE PHILISTINES

While all Israel knew that Samuel was God's prophet, all was not well with Israel. A powerfully threatening military force settled adjacent to Israel on the Mediterranean coast of Southwest Palestine. The Philistines were able to forge iron into weapons and controlled the weapons trade, holding a strategic advantage over Israel (see 1 Samuel 13:19-22).

Amos 9:7 identifies their migration from "Caphtor," which might be the island of Crete.[1] Israel battled them twice in 1 Samuel 4. The first battle ended in defeat, where Israel lost about four thousand men (1 Samuel 4:2). In the second battle, Israel supposed that bringing the ark of the covenant with them would ensure victory. The object of their trust was transferred from Jehovah to something material—idolatry.

3. IDOLATRY

Fill in the blanks

1 Samuel 4:3:
"And when the people had come into the camp, the elders of Israel said, 'Why has the LORD _____ us today before the Philistines? Let us bring the _____ of the _____ of the LORD from Shiloh to us, that when it comes among us _____ may _____ us from the hand of our enemies.'"

Evidently, they thought having a holy piece of furniture from the tabernacle would save them. Perhaps they thought that Jehovah God would have to

[1] *The New Unger's Bible Dictionary*, p. 1003. ©1988.

deliver the enemy into their hands or risk the ark being captured. This thinking shows the influence of idol-worshiping nations—trusting in something that was not God.

Israel may have thought they could force God's hand to save them, but they soon learned you cannot play chess with God. Not only did Israel suffer a severe blow in losing thirty thousand foot soldiers, but they also lost the ark. The two sons of Eli, Hophni and Phinehas, also died. This dreadful news brought about Eli's death, too. After judging Israel for forty years, he fell off his chair, breaking his neck and dying at age ninety-eight (1 Samuel 4:15-18).

The Philistines brought the ark into the house of their god, Dagon. However, in the morning, they found their idol had fallen on its face. The second day, Dagon fell again, where the head and both palms of his hands broke off. The Lord also caused an outbreak of tumors upon the Philistines. They recognized that it was "His hand" and not merely the ark's presence (1 Samuel 6:3). This led them to send the ark back to Israel.

Before the Philistines returned the ark to Israel they made golden images of the tumors and rats that ravaged their land as a "trespass offering" to go with the ark to test against mere chance and coincdence. These Gentiles were not under the Law of Moses, and they didn't know how to deal with Jehovah. However, even they recognized that they had trespassed against Him. They believed that these tumors were put upon them as the plagues were placed upon Egypt (1 Samuel 6:6). They made a new cart, set the ark on the cart, hitched it to two milk cows that were never yoked, and sent them away; with no driver, the cows were sent away with the ark. Only by direct intervention by God would the cows work together and return the ark to the right place. It is not natural for cows that have never been yoked to instantly work well with each other. Further still, it is very unnatural for milk cows

> So they said, "If you **send away** the **ark** of the **God of Israel**, do not send it **empty**; but by all means return it to Him with a **trespass offering**. Then you will be **healed**, and it will be known to you why **His hand** is not removed from you."
>
> - 1 Samuel 6:3

to be separated from their calves and not seek to be reunited with them. Therefore, if these cows worked together, walked in a straight line to Beth Shemesh, and left their calves behind, then it would necessarily imply that the God of Israel had done this. The cows broke from nature and walked a straight line to Beth Shemesh, lowing as they went (1 Samuel 6:12).

4. IRREVERENT CURIOSITY

The fourth enemy of Israel was a lack of proper fear. Upon the cows arriving, the people received the ark, took the cows, and made an offering to the Lord. The Levites carried the ark. They were the only ones permitted to bear it under the Law of Moses (Deuteronomy 10:8). However, the people trespassed and looked inside the ark of the covenant, something they were not permitted to do (1 Samuel 6:19). Back in Moses' day, the people were strictly warned not to break through and gaze upon the Lord (Exodus 19:21). The people should have learned, as Aaron and his sons did, that those who come near God must be reverent and regard Him as holy (Leviticus 9:24-10:7).

> So the children of Israel **put away** the **Baals** and the **Ashtoreths**, and served the **Lord only**.
>
> - 1 Samuel 7:4

Samuel walks the people back to God (1 Samuel 7:3-17)

Read 1 Samuel 7:3-4. Samuel addressed the enemies of Israel, and it started with their relationship with the Lord. What did this require?

- They had departed from Him and needed to "return to the LORD with all their hearts." I must love the Lord with all my heart, or I do not love Him enough.

Fill in the blanks

"You shall _____ the LORD your God with _____ your _____, with _____ your soul, and with _____ your strength" (Deuteronomy 6:5).

"He who _____ father or mother more than _____ is not _____ of _____. And he who _____ son or daughter more than Me is not _____ of Me" (Matthew 10:37).

- They had to put away the foreign gods. The Baals and Ashtoreths were false gods.
- They had to prepare their hearts for the Lord. A person prepares his heart by having a feeling of sorrow for sin and a willingness to listen to the truth to obey it.

Questions

9. Where was Samuel's home (1 Samuel 7:17)? _____

10. How many lords did the Philistines have (1 Samuel 6:16)? _____

11. Why did none of Samuel's words "fall to the ground," or fail to be true (1 Samuel 3:19)?_____

12. Is God's word always right (Psalm 19:7-9)? _____

13. What is the great commandment, and what does it mean? See Mark 12:29, 30._____

Conclusion

The people listened, removed the idols, and served the Lord only. When the Philistines came against them again, the people asked Samuel to continually cry out to the Lord, that "He may save us" (1 Samuel 7:8). This clearly shows that the reforms Samuel did were real. Before, they reasoned that the ark may save them by being carried into battle (1 Samuel 4:3). Now, their confidence was in the Lord. The Lord protected them by bringing unusually loud thunder, which confused the Philistines (1 Samuel 7:10). Their enemy was driven back and subdued. So effective was this that they did not come into the territory of Israel anymore, and Israel recovered their cities which were taken. Samuel took a stone, set it up, and called it Ebenezer, saying, "Thus far the Lord has helped us" (1 Samuel 7:12).

Lesson 2
Walking With Saul: A King Like the Nations

I was born to Kish, of the tribe of Benjamin. I led a life in agriculture and grew to be the tallest man in Israel. One day forever changed my life. When my father's donkeys were lost, he sent me to look for them. What I found on that journey while searching for what was lost ended in a surprise: I was anointed king of the country through none other than Samuel the prophet! I started out well but was overcome by fear and envy. I am Saul, a king like the nations of the world. *Come walk with me in my history.*

The year is around 1053 BC. The nation of Israel is still threatened and oppressed by the Philistines. Samuel is now a lot older. Despite him working hard to bring about godly reforms in Israel, his children are corrupt and have chased after dishonest gain while perverting justice (1 Samuel 8:3). Samuel's firstborn, Joel, means, "Jehovah is God." His second son, Abijah, means, "Jehovah is Father." Sadly, they did not live up to their names, nor did they follow Samuel's example. Rather, they "turned aside" after error.

KEY PASSAGE

...and said to him, "Look, you are **old**, and your sons do not walk in your ways. Now make us a **king** to judge us like all the **nations**."

- 1 Samuel 8:5

The value of children and godly training

As a young person, be very aware that people are watching you and taking note of your example whether it is good or bad. Your manner of life will have a direct effect on your siblings and parents. Samuel's children chose to live in a way that brought dishonor to the Lord. Aware of this, the people began a movement, asking Samuel to install a king like the ones they saw the other nations had. Long before, God told Abraham, "I will make you exceedingly fruitful; and I will make nations of you, and kings shall come from you" (Genesis 17:6). He also spoke in Genesis 17:16 regarding Sarah, "kings of peoples shall be from her." The problem was the kind of king they wanted and their rejection of God as king. After Samuel taught the people of the perils of having a king like the nations, they refused to heed the warning (1 Samuel 8:19).

The Bible instructs children to be of good behavior, to protect the heart, and to consider the example they set.

Fill in the blanks

Psalm 119:9
"BETH. How can a _____ _____ cleanse his way? By _____ heed according to Your _____."

Psalm 127:4-5
"Like _____ in the hand of a _____, So are the _____ of one's youth. _____ is the man who has his quiver full of them; They shall not be _____, But shall speak with their _____ in the gate."

Children are pictured as arrows—effective, long-range weapons of war. Arrows must be crafted with care so that when they are shot, they go to their target with great accuracy. From the father's training, children are crafted to meet life's challenges. When fathers fail or are hampered in

> Nevertheless the people **refused** to **obey** the voice of **Samuel**; and they said, "No, but we will have a **king** over us."
>
> - 1 Samuel 8:19

LESSON 2 Walking With Saul: A King Like the Nations

training children correctly, disastrous consequences can follow. In Titus 1:5-7, God requires overseers of the local church to have faithful children. These are children who are obedient to the Lord. Likewise, the overseer must not have children accused of "dissipation" or "insubordination." This simply means, "...They must not be known as children who are wild and who do not obey."[1] Children who grow up unruly cripple the father's reputation and ability to lead others. Both Samuel's house and Eli's house shared this unfortunate problem.

Read 1 Samuel 8 to find the answers.

True or false

1. **T or F**   Samuel's sons were terrible judges.
2. **T or F**   Samuel was pleased with the people asking for a king.
3. **T or F**   When Israel asked for a king, they were rejecting God as their king.
4. **T or F**   Samuel taught the people that if they had a king, he would take 15% of their produce and sheep.

Saul, son of Kish

In the year 1051 BC, Saul becomes king of Israel and will reign 40 years. Saul is the first of three kings in the period of Old Testament history described as the United Kingdom. This was the time when all the tribes of Israel were under the rule of one king. The rule of judges ends with Saul. Saul is the son of Kish, from the tribe of Benjamin. He is described as a very handsome man as well as a very tall man. In fact, he was the tallest man in Israel! He was taller than any of the people from his shoulders upward (1 Samuel 9:2; 10:23). Saul's gigantic physical appearance would fit him to be a king like the nations. He became a big and strong warrior. However, the people will learn that the stature of a man does not define the stature of his rule. Someone once said, "You don't measure size with a ruler, you don't figure height with a yardstick, and you never judge a man by how tall he looks in a mirror. The giant is as he does."[2]

Saul's beginning presence on the biblical scene is interesting. When his father's donkeys strayed, Saul went on a quest to find them with his servant. They passed through the mountains of Ephraim and back to Benjamin and finally arrived in the land of Zuph. This was a journey that had taken about three days. Considerately, Saul began to worry that his father

---

[1] See Titus 1:6 of the *International Children's Bible*
[2] Newman, Joseph M., dir. *The Twilight Zone*. Season 5, episode 5, "The Last Night of a Jockey." Aired October 25, 1963, on CBS.

was now worried (1 Samuel 9:5, 20). It is very telling of the ignorance of Saul that despite Samuel's reputation, Saul was not aware of who he was or that he lived fairly close by; however, Saul's servant knew about him (1 Samuel 9:6, 18)! Further, Saul had nothing to give Samuel, but again, the servant is the one with the money (1 Samuel 9:7-8). Further still, we see Saul taking the advice of his servant, the one under him (1 Samuel 9:9-10).

We quickly learn that Samuel already knew Saul was approaching (1 Samuel 9:16). God was working to bring Saul and Samuel together without destroying Saul's free will. After meeting Saul, Samuel explained that the nation's desire was for him to become king. The next morning, Samuel anointed Saul as king with a flask of oil (1 Samuel 10:1). On his way home, Saul began to prophesy, which surprised the people; they knew him for his physical ability, but not his spirituality: "Is Saul also among the prophets?" (1 Samuel 10:11-12). Saul's uncle, possibly Abner (see 1 Samuel 14:50), met Saul and his servant, inquiring where they went. They told him they met Samuel but didn't reveal what Samuel said. Samuel then called the people together at Mizpah, where he selected Benjamin of all the tribes of Israel. From Benjamin, he selected the family of Matri. He then chose Saul, the son of Kish. However, Saul was not there but was hidden among the equipment (1 Samuel 10:22-23).

The trials of Saul

THE TESTING OF PRIDE BY REBELS (1 SAMUEL 10:27)

As king, Saul was quickly tested. Samuel explained the behavior of royalty but there were some rebels who despised Saul, asking, "How can this man save us?" (1 Samuel 10:27). Saul showed that he could hold his peace and not harbor a grudge (1 Samuel 11:12-13). Humility can be a tremendous ally for a ruler!

Fill in the blanks

Leviticus 19:18
"You shall not take _____, nor _____ any _____ against the children of your people, but you shall _____ your neighbor as _____: I am the LORD."

THE TESTING OF LEADERSHIP BY THE AMMONITES (1 SAMUEL 11)

Saul was tested again with an oppressive enemy encamped against Jabesh Gilead (1 Samuel 11). The Ammonites were rivals during the days of Jephthah and acted deceitfully in an attempt to retake old territories (Judges 11:13). In Saul's day, they were up to no good again, wanting to

LESSON 2 Walking With Saul: A King Like the Nations

subdue the people of Jabesh and bring reproach upon Israel by putting out their right eyes. Messengers from Jabesh went to see if anyone would save them, which settled great sadness upon the people. Resuming the life of a farmer, Saul heard the people weeping while he was plowing in the field. After learning Ammon's plot, the Spirit of God came upon him, and his anger was greatly aroused. With the graphic action of cutting up oxen, he rallied the nation to come to battle. The turnout was numerically great; three hundred thousand from Israel and thirty thousand from Judah rallied to him. This crisis, with Saul's leadership, united a nation. He valiantly delivered Jabesh Gilead from the Ammonites. He maintained his humility by sparing those who previously despised him, after which he was nationally recognized as king in Gilgal (1 Samuel 11:15). This was Saul's finest moment.

Questions

5. The Ammonites were distant relatives to Israel. Do you know how (Genesis 19:38)? _____

6. In pursuing his father's lost donkeys, who did Saul meet? _____

7. What did Saul learn from this meeting? _____

8. What people did Saul first save? _____

9. Who did Saul recognize as the deliverer (1 Samuel 11:13)? _____

10. What promise did Samuel make to the people and the king (see 1 Samuel 12:14-15)? _____

11. What did Samuel want the people to consider (see 1 Samuel 12:24)? _____

12. What are some great things God has done for you? _____

> And afterward they asked for a **king**; so God gave them **Saul** the son of Kish, a man of the tribe of Benjamin, for **forty years**.
>
> - Acts 13:21

THE TESTING OF FAITH BY THE PHILISTINES (1 SAMUEL 13)

In Saul's second year, he failed the demands of faith. Israel was severely outmanned by the Philistine army. There was no blacksmith in all of Israel and therefore no real weapons of war that could be forged, and the Philistines wanted to keep it that way (1 Samuel 13:19-23). Saul confessed that God had brought about salvation over the Ammonites, but that reliance was now lost. His army consisted of only three thousand men. God could have delivered him with only three hundred men if he trusted in Him. After a skirmish with a Philistine garrison in Geba, the Philistines came against him with thirty thousand chariots, six thousand horsemen, and people as numerous as the sand of the seashore. Distressed, many Israelites hid in caves, thickets, etc. Saul's army further dwindled to six hundred (1 Samuel 13:17). He was told to wait for Samuel's arrival to sacrifice. However, when Samuel delayed and the people scattered, he felt compelled to break the law and burn a sacrifice to the Lord. He was rebuked by Samuel: His kingdom would not continue on but would be given to a man after God's own heart (1 Samuel 13:13-14). Fear is the enemy of faith. In this account, Saul feared the size of the enemy but didn't fear God!

THE TESTING OF PRIDE AND OBEDIENCE BY THE AMALEKITES (1 SAMUEL 15)

Saul gained some independence against Israel's enemies by harassing them (1 Samuel 14:47-48). He was put to the test again when he was ordered to utterly destroy Amalek, not sparing any person or animal (1 Samuel 15:1-4). These were barbaric people, yet Saul only partially obeyed—sparing the wicked king, Agag, and the best of the sheep and oxen. Pride had settled into Saul's heart and changed him. He erected a monument for himself in Carmel (1 Samuel 15:12). He boasted to Samuel

LESSON 2 Walking With Saul: A King Like the Nations

that he obeyed the Lord, about which Samuel asked, "What then is the bleating of the sheep in my ears and the lowing of the oxen which I hear?" (1 Samuel 15:14). Partial obedience is never obedience! Saul responded that the people spared these to offer a sacrifice to the Lord in Gilgal (1 Samuel 15:21). However, God doesn't accept property gained by sin as a sacrifice. Samuel admonished, "Behold, to obey is better than sacrifice, And to heed than the fat of rams" (1 Samuel 15:22). It might have seemed efficient to Saul but not to God. Saul's actions were faithless by rejecting the word of the Lord (1 Samuel 15:26; Romans 10:17). We should never place what we think to be good on the same level as what God has commanded.

Questions

13. What three reasons did Saul have for offering an unlawful sacrifice (1 Samuel 13:11-12)? _____

14. Did any of these reasons make Saul's actions okay (1 Samuel 13:13)? _____

15. What is better than sacrifices? _____

16. What are some reasons people have today for offering wrong worship to God? _____

17. Are there any right reasons to do something that is wrong in and of itself? _____

18. What did the Lord command Saul to utterly destroy (1 Samuel 15:3)? _____

19. What did Saul not destroy (1 Samuel 15:8-9)? _____

20. Is partial obedience acceptable to God (1 Samuel 15:10-11)? _____

21. What are some ways people partially obey their parents today and are still disobedient? _____
_____
_____
_____

22. What ways may some partially obey God today and still be disobedient?
_____
_____
_____
_____

Conclusion

Walking with Saul is a walk through paths of pride. Saul was led by fear, not faith. Saul was consumed with jealousy, not joy. Depression pursued even as he hunted down David, one of his most skilled warriors, to try to kill him. Near his end, Saul became so misguided that he consulted a witch to contact dead Samuel (1 Samuel 28). Saul's final stand was to perish with his sons in a heated battle with the Philistines. Severely wounded, and not wanting to be delivered into their hands, he committed suicide (1 Samuel 31:4). Sacrifice is dying for a selfless purpose (as Jesus died to set us free); suicide, however, is dying for a selfish end. A proud, envious, self-centered life is a dangerous way to live! The brave men of Jabesh Gilead returned a favor to Saul, traveling all night to rescue the lifeless bodies of Saul and his sons (1 Samuel 31:11-13).

Lesson 3
Walking With David: A King After God's Own Heart

I am the son of Jesse the Bethlehemite, and the great-grandson of Boaz the husband of Ruth (1 Samuel 16:1; Ruth 4:17). I am the youngest brother in my family, having seven older brothers (1 Samuel 16:10-11). My occupation was a shepherd, so I would tend my father's sheep in the field. Sometimes, predators would prey upon them, but the Lord was with me in delivering them. I continued as a shepherd until one day, the great prophet Samuel visited my father's house; he called me out to anoint me king over Israel during the reign of Saul. As for Saul, I would not lay my hand against the Lord's anointed.

One day, a giant of a man from Gath named Goliath came out and mocked Saul and the armies of the living God. Gath was one of the principal cities of the Philistines and had a long history of giants living in the city (Joshua 11:22). Many years after Goliath, when I was ruling as a king, another giant arose from Gath and began to taunt Israel. He had twenty-four fingers and toes, six on each hand

KEY PASSAGE
But the LORD said to Samuel, "Do not look at his **appearance** or at the **height** of his stature, because I have **refused** him. For the LORD **does not see** as man sees; for man looks at the **outward** appearance, but the LORD looks at the **heart**."

- 1 Samuel 16:7

> And when He had removed him, He **raised up** for them **David** as king, to whom also He gave testimony and said, "I have found David the son of Jesse, **a man after My own heart**, who will do all My will."
>
> - Acts 13:22

and six on each foot. My nephew, Jonathan, took courage and slew him (1 Chronicles 20:6-8). Goliath was a skilled champion warrior, whose height was well over nine feet tall! His presence and words sent waves of fear throughout my people. He was a sight to behold. However, I knew that God would deliver him into my hand as He delivered the bear and the lion that came against my father's sheep. With my sling, I sunk a stone deep into his forehead. After he dropped, I took his own sword and cut off his head (1 Samuel 17:33-51). This sent fear into the Philistines, and God gave us a tremendous victory that day. God blessed me with so many victories against Israel's enemies that the womenfolk sang a song in the streets: "Saul has slain his thousands, And David his ten thousands" (1 Samuel 18:7). Although this caused Saul to despise me—and he even tried to kill me—yet he made me a captain over a thousand men (1 Samuel 18:13). After I married Saul's daughter, Michal, Saul became obsessed with trying to kill me. He even tried to pin me to the wall with his spear—a threat I barely escaped; there was but a step between me and death. However, my best friend was Saul's son Jonathan. Jonathan was a loyal friend who defended me before his father. Looking into Jonathan, I saw the dearest of friends on earth. I mourned greatly at his death.

Although I destroyed Goliath, escaped the death snares of Saul, and delivered Israel from all of her enemies through the grace of God, I was brought low by an enemy within, one that resided in my heart: the enemy of lust. I multiplied wives to myself, which itself was not lawful (Deuteronomy 17:17; 2 Samuel 5:13). Then, in a season of idleness and ease, I stayed behind and saw my neighbor's wife, coveted her, and took her. I tried to deceive her husband and the world but was only veiled in my own deception. I didn't know that this decision would carry with it so many consequences and take me into places of sadness, fear, guilt, and despair. "Blessed is the man to whom the LORD does not impute iniquity, And in whose spirit there is no deceit" (Psalm 32:2). Hiding this sin even affected my physical health. "When I kept silent, my bones grew old Through my groaning all the day long. For day and night Your hand was heavy upon me; My vitality was turned into the drought of summer. Selah" (Psalm 32:3-4). God's prophet, Nathan, made me see the error of my ways and brought me back to the pathway of God's forgiveness and grace. "I acknowledged my sin to You, And my iniquity I have not hidden. I said, 'I will confess my transgressions to the LORD,' And You forgave the iniquity of my sin. Selah" (Psalm 32:5). However, the rest of my life on earth was forever changed by that one night I chose to lust after a beautiful woman. My name is David. *Come walk with me in my history.*

David's courage in war (1 Samuel 17)

David was a man after God's own heart, but he was not a sinless man. We admire his courage to face the champion warrior Goliath, who was likely around 9.5 feet tall, wore a coat of mail that weighed 125 pounds, and wielded a spear with an iron spearhead weighing 15 pounds! David confidently ran to defeat Goliath without a sword, crediting that God would give him the victory (1 Samuel 17:47-48). We often refer to this section as "David and Goliath," but it is really about David and Saul. Saul was the king of Israel and, physically, the biggest man in Israel. He should have gone out to battle Goliath as a shepherd over God's sheep. The difference between the two men was that Saul trusted in worldly armor and strength, while David trusted in the Lord. Read 1 Samuel 17:32-40.

Questions

1. Why did David say, "Let no man's heart fail"? _____
   _____

2. What was Saul's response to David's offer to go fight Goliath? _____
   _____
   _____

3. From what did David draw as the source of his confidence to destroy Goliath (17:34-37)? _____

4. Do you see any evidence of the Lord's care in your life? _____

5. What did Saul trust in and try to equip David with (17:38)? By contrast, in what did David trust? _____
   _____
   _____

> For though we walk in the **flesh**, we do not **war** according to the flesh. For the **weapons** of our warfare are not **carnal** but mighty in **God** for pulling down **strongholds**...
>
> - 2 Corinthians 10:3-4

6. What is the Christian's battle today, and what is the armor that soldiers of Christ wear? See 2 Corinthians 10:3-6 and Ephesians 6:10-20.

_____
_____
_____
_____
_____

There are two different ways one could look at Goliath. One is, "He is so big that he could never be killed." The other is, "He is so big that we cannot miss."

David's house (2 Samuel 7)

When the Lord gave David rest from all of his enemies, David desired to build God a house. He recognized that he lived in a fine house of cedar, but the ark of God dwelt in a tent. David's heart was in the right place; however, a very important lesson comes to us. While David's intentions were good, God asked David an important question.

Fill in the blanks

2 Samuel 7:7
"Wherever I have _____ about with all the children of Israel, _____ I ever _____ a _____ to _____ from the _____ of Israel, whom I _____ to shepherd My people Israel, saying, '_____ have you not _____ Me a _____ of _____?'"

This question is important regarding the authority of the word of God and man's permission to act. If a man should have acted to build God a house of cedar, then God would have had to ask, or command, "a house" of "cedar" to be built. No one can act presumptuously to do something for God when He is silent on the matter. We can learn what God wants in three ways. First, when He commands us to do something or states that something should be done. God stated that man must believe and be baptized in order to be saved (Mark 16:16). Second, when He gives us an example that is approved by Him. Jesus told the apostles, "I have given you an example, that you should do as I have done to you" (John 13:15). Paul said, "Imitate me, just as I imitate Christ." Third, by a necessary inference, which is an inescapable conclusion. We know that we are to partake of the Lord's Supper on the first day of the week because of the example of Paul with the Lord's church at Troas in Acts 20:7. But we also know that we are to do that every first day of the week from the inescapable conclusion that whenever there was a first day of the week, the disciples came together to break the bread of the Lord's Supper.

Questions

7. At first, did Nathan the prophet think it was okay for David to build God a house? Read 2 Samuel 7:3. What do you think Nathan should have done first before answering David? See the principle in Deuteronomy 17:8-9.

   _____
   _____

8. Since God had never commanded or authorized any man to build Him a house, did David have permission to go ahead and build Him one anyway? Read 1 Chronicles 17:3-4. _____

9. Why would God not allow David to build Him a house? Read 1 Chronicles 22:7-8. _____
   _____

10. Who would build God a house? Read 1 Chronicles 22:9-10. _____
    _____

While David would not build God a house of cedar, God would build David a house of kings. The "house of David" was a dynasty of kings descending from David (2 Samuel 7:11-17). For years, skeptics charged that David was simply a made-up king of biblical lore.

In 1993, archeologists dug up historical evidence of the "house of David," mentioned in an inscription on the Tel Dan Stele. This inscription refers to a battle several generations after David lived and is dated to the ninth century. It proves

Oren Rozen (https://commons.wikimedia.org/wiki/File:JRSLM 300116 Tel Dan Stele 01.jpg), https://creativecommons.org/licenses/by-sa/4.0/legalcode

that David had a house of kings and was the founder of his empire. Biblical history is real history!

Stele: "an upright stone slab or pillar bearing an inscription or design and serving as a monument, marker, or the like."[1]

Jesus is from the "house of David," and the blessings promised to David are ultimately anchored in Jesus Christ, the King of kings and Son of David (see Luke 1:26-33).

David's failure when at ease (2 Samuel 11)

When kings went out to war, David stayed in Jerusalem (2 Samuel 11:1). In a season of ease, David fell to sin. Idleness and ease can make it easy to fall prey to sin. Paul warned of widows casting off their faith, learning to become idle, and turning into gossips and busybodies (1 Timothy 5:12-13). If idleness could become a snare to David—a king, warrior, and psalmist—it can become a snare to anyone. God's solution is to be busy in good things (2 Thessalonians 3:10; Ephesians 4:28).

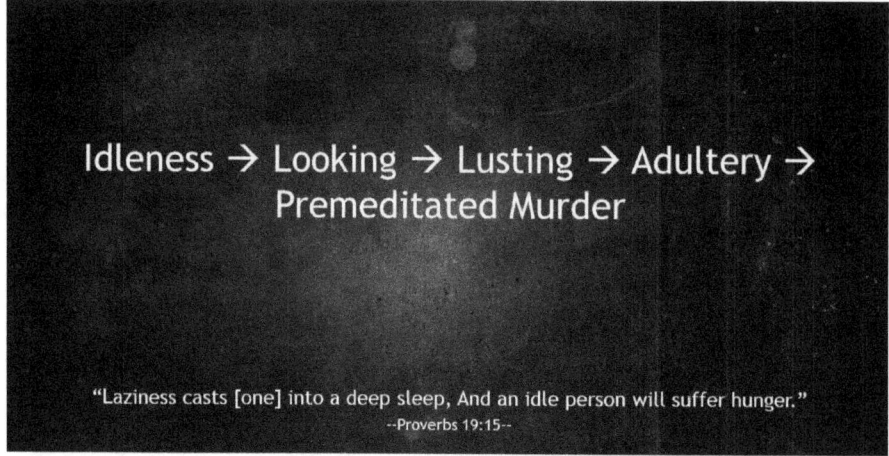

Idleness → Looking → Lusting → Adultery → Premeditated Murder

"Laziness casts [one] into a deep sleep, And an idle person will suffer hunger."
--Proverbs 19:15--

Not only did David fall into sin, but his sin continued to grow, like a rolling snowball down a mountainside. From idleness, he lusted after another man's wife. Then, he took her and committed adultery with her. After this, he acted deceitfully to her husband, Uriah. One night, he even worked to get Uriah drunk. And when this didn't get what David wanted, he sent a message in Uriah's hand to Joab, the commanding officer. The letter said to send Uriah into a hot battle with the enemy and to pull away so that Uriah would die. How tragic and corrupt David had become! In fact, one could say that the Gentile, Uriah, was more how David used to be while David was the one living like a godless Gentile.

[1] Dictionary.com

LESSON 3 Walking With David: A King After God's Own Heart

DAVID (Beloved)
- A Judean
- A mighty warrior
- Exercised self-restraint
- Thoughtful of the ark
- Thoughtful of Israel and Judah
- Thoughtful of his fellow soldiers and commanding officer
- A faithful messenger

DAVID WAS A MAN AFTER GOD'S OWN HEART

URIAH (Jehovah is my light)
- A Gentile
- A mighty warrior
- Exercised self-restraint
- Thoughtful of the ark
- Thoughtful of Israel and Judah
- Thoughtful of his fellow soldiers and commanding officer
- A faithful messenger

URIAH BECAME EVERYTHING DAVID ONCE WAS

For many months, David tried to cover his sin with a veil of deception. Finally, he was rebuked by Nathan the prophet in a powerful parable that brought righteousness and justice squarely before David's eyes (2 Samuel 12:1-15). David repented and was instantly forgiven by God. However, God would allow severe consequences to remain. Some of those included the death of his son and the continued adversity arising in his own house. David's life was never the same after he sinned with Bathsheba.

This saying is true: "Sin will take you farther than you ever expected to go, it will keep you longer than you ever intended to stay, and it will cost you more than you ever expected to pay."

Questions

11. According to Proverbs 6:32-33, what does a man lack when he commits adultery? What does he do to his soul? What will he get?

   _____
   _____
   _____

12. According to Proverbs 23:32-35, who has sorrow and complaints? What does Solomon say not to do? What kind of bite is alcohol like?

   _____
   _____
   _____

13. List some good things to pray about from David's Psalm (see Psalm 19:12-14). _____
   _____
   _____
   _____

Conclusion

While sin can be forgiven by God's gracious mercy, we should know that prevention is cheaper than redemption. We should pray fervently to keep both mouth and mind acceptable in God's sight.

Lesson 4
Walking With Solomon: A King After God's Own Heart

The United Kingdom

Saul > David > Solomon

Nature: A king who pursued wisdom
Date: 970 B.C – 930 B.C.
Tribe: Judah

My mother was Bathsheba. My father was a great king and mighty warrior whom God used to bring down surrounding nations. With him were thirty-seven of the strongest warriors I've ever known (2 Samuel 23:8-39). It was a relief to know these men were on our side. One fearsome warrior, Josheb-Basshebeth was exceedingly militant. He was called Adino the Eznite because he killed eight hundred men at one time! Another man, Eleazar the Ahohite, refused to retreat from the Philistines when others did but arose and pressed the attack against them. He wielded the sword so well and for so long that his hand stuck to his sword! Other scenes like these could be spoken of. It didn't matter if the enemy was numerous or had spectacular, giant-sized warriors; no matter what, they fell before my father and his mighty men. My father knew that God was the One who gave him these victories and that He gave Israel rest from our enemies.

KEY PASSAGE

But **Solomon** built Him a **house**.

- Acts 7:47

Before he died, my father made great preparations for the temple of Jehovah (1 Chronicles 22:3-5). Besides preparing the materials for nails and stones, he acquired one hundred thousand talents of gold and one million talents of silver (1 Chronicles 22:14). God showed my father David what he wanted, and these things were written down (1 Chronicles 28:12, 19). Because my father was a man of war and shed much blood, God didn't permit him to build the temple but rather chose me, a man of rest, to have this privilege (1 Chronicles 22:6-10).

Yet, I was young, raw, and inexperienced; I lacked the experience necessary to be a king—let alone a master builder of a temple that would be magnificent throughout the nations. My father instructed me in the way to be successful:

> "Only may the LORD give you wisdom and understanding, and give you charge concerning Israel, that you may keep the law of the LORD your God. Then you will prosper, if you take care to fulfill the statutes and judgments with which the LORD charged Moses concerning Israel. Be strong and of good courage; do not fear nor be dismayed" (1 Chronicles 22:12-13).

But how could I be courageous to do something which I felt unqualified to do? My father showed me the pathway by tying courageous confidence with wisdom and understanding. Wisdom and understanding he tied with keeping the law of the Lord that Moses gave. As my father instructed me, so Moses encouraged Joshua to "Be strong and of good courage" (Deuteronomy 31:7-8). If Joshua could complete his undertaking in bringing an entire nation into a land where giants ruled, surely with the same recipe for success, I could face the undertaking of building a glorious and magnificent temple to my God. My name is Solomon. I am the third king of Israel. *Come walk with me in my history!*

Questions

1. To be successful and to carry out his plans, what do you think Solomon's first quest should be? _____

2. How many mighty warriors did David have? _____

3. What did David advise Solomon to have in order to accomplish his work (1 Chronicles 22:12-13)? Name the positive things Solomon must find. And what should he guard against? _____

4. Who is the source of wisdom, and where can we find wisdom today? _____
_____
_____

Solomon's request for wisdom

Strength and courage are what Solomon needed to face the challenges of being a ruler and building the temple for the Lord God. Solomon began his rule with a great quality—humility. Moses taught that humility is a key component in being faithful to the Lord (Deuteronomy 8:1-3). As a young man, Solomon viewed himself as a small child who lacked the knowledge and experience to know how to conduct himself in the affairs of being king.

> "Now, O LORD my God, You have made Your servant king instead of my father David, but I am a little child; I do not know how to go out or come in" (1 Kings 3:7).

This is a tremendous trait for any young person to have and it was the foundation for Solomon becoming great! Solomon was not a child but considered himself to be inexperienced as a child and that is what enabled him to learn great things. David had already spoken of Solomon as being a wise man (see 1 Kings 2:9). Yet, Solomon was wise enough to understand that he lacked the sufficient knowledge needed. He also knew that God could provide that needed wisdom. Someone who is wise in their own opinion is not teachable. They will not listen to counsel from others. The New Testament warns Christians to have a humble view of themselves and to not chase after "high things."

Fill in the blanks

Romans 12:16
"Be of the same mind toward one another. Do _____ set your mind on _____ things, but _____ with the _____. Do not be _____ in your own _____."

> Only may the Lord give you **wisdom** and **understanding**, and give you charge concerning Israel, that you may **keep the law** of the Lord your God.
>
> - 1 Chronicles 22:12

Walking With Prophets and Kings

Colossians 3:1-2
"If then you were _____ with _____, seek those things which are _____, where Christ is, sitting at the right hand of God. Set your mind on _____ _____, not on things on the earth."

We ought not to set our minds on the high things of this life: those things that are grand, rich, powerful, and famed. However, we should be happy to associate with those who are humble and set our minds on things above, things that are in heaven where the King of kings reigns and where we will one day live.

As the first order in Solomon's administration, he chose to worship the Lord. He needed to read the Law of Moses and charted his course to make a trip to Gibeon. The history of Gibeon is rich! Long ago the people of this land deceitfully made a covenant with Joshua as he failed to consult God about them and believed their lies. Therefore, the Gibeonites were spared in the wake of Joshua's conquest of the nations. That covenant Joshua made with them was binding. Solomon's predecessor, Saul, had total disregard for it and sought to kill the Gibeonites in his zeal for Israel. This resulted in a three-year famine which would cost Saul's house seven lives to be hung in order to take away the blight (2 Samuel 21:2-14). If this covenant was binding although it was entered into deceptively, then how much more should the covenant God made with Israel be? At this time, the tabernacle that Moses built is stationed at Gibeon (2 Chronicles 1:3). Solomon went there and worshiped God for he wanted to be near God's tent and offer an abundant sacrifice to the God he loved. To his surprise, God appeared to Solomon in a dream and said, "Ask! What shall I give you?" (2 Chronicles 1:7; 1 Kings 3:5).

Read 1 Kings 3:4-15 and 2 Chronicles 1 and answer the following questions.

Questions

5. Who was Solomon and the assembly seeking at Gibeon? _____
   _____

6. How many burnt offerings did Solomon sacrifice? _____

7. Who appeared to Solomon in a dream at night? _____
   _____

8. What did Solomon ask for? What did he not ask for? What would you ask for if you were in Solomon's place? _____
   _____
   _____

LESSON 4 Walking With Solomon: A King Who Had It All 33

9. What effect did Solomon's speech have on God? _____
_____

10. What did God say He would give Solomon? _____
_____

11. What did God say Solomon must do if he wanted to have length of days? _____
_____

12. Where did Solomon go after he departed from Gibeon and what did he do? _____
_____

Applications

13. The need for humility. The first step that led to Solomon's great success was having a humble heart. As a king, Solomon referred to himself as a "little child" (1 Kings 3:7). This means he viewed himself as inexperienced and wanted to gain knowledge so that he could reign as a righteous leader.

    a. What did Jesus say we must become in order to enter the kingdom of heaven (Matthew 18:3-4). What does this mean in your own words? _____
    _____
    _____

    b. What is the condition of a person who views himself to be wiser than others (Proverbs 26:12)? _____
    _____

    c. What does the Bible say to a person who thinks he knows it all and what does the Bible say we should not think (see 1 Corinthians 8:2; Romans 12:3)? _____
    _____
    _____

14. How can we display humility in our lives:

    a. To our parents? _____
    _____
    _____

b. To our siblings? _____
   _____
   _____
   _____

   c. To gospel preachers and teachers? _____
   _____
   _____
   _____

15. Have you prayed for wisdom (James 1:5)?
   _____

Solomon's success

Solomon became a great king. He reigned and built things with great wisdom. He had wise decisions in his judgments. You can read of an example in his ability to judge between two women who both claimed to be the mother of the same child (1 Kings 3:16-28). Who should he believe? Solomon easily found out who the real mother was. In his wisdom, he spoke 3,000 proverbs and 1,005 songs (1 Kings 4:32). We have several of his proverbs in the book of Proverbs. We have one song in the Song of Solomon.

Solomon was a builder. He had thousands and thousands of men working for him. He built the temple of God in seven years (1 Kings 6:38). The furnishings of the temple can be read about in 1 Kings 6. The temple was built on Mount Moriah (2 Chronicles 3:1). Recall how God appeared to Abraham hundreds of years earlier and commanded him to go to the land of Moriah and offer his only son on one of the mountains which God would tell him (Genesis 22:1-2). Solomon built the temple of God in this area. Years later, God would send His Son to teach and eventually be put to death in this very area for our sins! Solomon became very famous and people from all over the earth sought his presence (1 Kings 10:23-25). He became great in trade and even built merchant ships which would bring abundant wealth every

> If any of you lacks **wisdom**, let him **ask** of God, who gives to all **liberally** and without reproach, and it **will be given** to him.
>
> - James 1:5

LESSON 4 Walking With Solomon: A King Who Had It All 35

three years of gold, silver, ivory, apes, and monkeys (1 Kings 10:22). He built a strong military that had one thousand four hundred chariots and twelve thousand horsemen (1 Kings 10:26). He and his administration became exceedingly wealthy where silver was as common as stones (1 Kings 10:27). None of his drinking vessels were silver—all were gold (1 Kings 10:21).

True or false

16. **T or F**   Solomon built the temple in eleven years (1 Kings 6:38).

17. **T or F**   Solomon built the temple according to the plans given to him.

18. **T or F**   The temple was going to be famous and glorious throughout all the countries (1 Chronicles 22:5).

19. **T or F**   The queen of Sheba heard of Solomon's fame and came to question him with hard questions (1 Kings 10:1).

20. **T or F**   The queen of Sheba stumped Solomon with some very difficult questions (1 Kings 10:3).

21. **T or F**   Solomon spent thirteen years building his own house (1 Kings 7:1).

22. **T or F**   Solomon was so rich, that he made gold and silver as common as stones (2 Chronicles 9:27).

23. **T or F**   God appeared to Solomon many times in his lifetime (1 Kings 11:9).

Solomon's tragic failure

Solomon loved many women and married seven hundred princesses (1 Kings 11:1-3). In addition, he accumulated three hundred concubines. A concubine is an inferior wife. Not only did Solomon violate the original pattern for a marriage as taught in Genesis 2 of one man bound to one woman, but he also allowed the religions of these women to turn his heart away from God and to false idols (1 Kings 11:4-6). This angered the Lord who then made a judgment against Solomon and his kingdom. See 1 Kings 11:11-12.

Fill in the blanks

"Therefore the LORD said to Solomon, 'Because you have done this, and have not kept My _____ and My _____, which I have _____ you, I will surely _____ the _____ away from you and give it to your servant. Nevertheless I will not do it in your days, for the sake of your father David; I will _____ it out of the hand of your son."

Conclusion

Although God gave Solomon wisdom, wisdom must be kept and used for good. Solomon himself said, "...Keep sound wisdom and discretion" (Proverbs 3:21). The Bible doesn't teach that once one is wise, he is always wise. He can lose his wisdom by departing from the very thing that makes him wise—the word of God.

Walking With Rehoboam and Jeroboam: A Kingdom Divides

Rehoboam, the son of Solomon

During the reign of David and Solomon, the kingdom of Israel was in its glorious golden years. It was the only period of Israel's kingdom years where strong political unification existed, where the land that was promised to Abraham was controlled, where the greatest material prosperity was enjoyed, and where the greatest spiritual strength was found. This, however, began to fade during my father's declining years and was lost during my reign as king. Solomon had become consumed with the love of women and fell into idolatry (1 Kings 11:1-5). As a result, God passed judgment that ten tribes would be taken away from him and given to another man who would become my own adversary.

In 930 B.C., I became king at the age of forty-one years old and reigned for only seventeen years (1 Kings 14:21). My mother's name is Naamah, from the nation of Ammon. The Ammonites did not fear Jehovah but worshiped Milcom, or as some called him, Molech (1 Kings 11:5). My mother, along with my father's other wives influenced him to honor various national gods (1 Kings 11:7-8). Presently, my nation is given to idolatry (1 Kings 14:21-23).

You could describe my time like that of a man dancing on the top of a volcano! There was a lot of discontent and unhappiness in Israel that was ready to blow up in a fiery fury, one that would forever divide us into bitter rivals! To make matters worse, I didn't ask God for wisdom, I allowed pride to interfere with sound reason, and I rejected the advice of older and wiser men.

KEY PASSAGE

So **Shishak** king of Egypt came up against **Jerusalem**, and took away the treasures of the **house of the LORD** and the treasures of the **king's house**; he took **everything**. He also carried away the **gold shields** which Solomon had made.

- 2 Chronicles 12:9

My father expressed his misgivings concerning me when he penned in Ecclesiastes 2:18-19:

> "Then I hated all my labor in which I had toiled under the sun, because I must leave it to the man who will come after me. And who knows whether he will be wise or a fool? Yet he will rule over all my labor in which I toiled and in which I have shown myself wise under the sun. This also is vanity" (Ecclesiastes 2:18-19).

My name is Rehoboam. I am the fourth king of Judah. *Come walk with me in my history!*

Proud and poor discernment (1 Kings 12:1–20)

Rehoboam came to the throne in troublesome times. The people chose the city of Shechem rather than the capital, Jerusalem, to make Rehoboam king (1 Kings 12:1). They were unsure if they wanted to continue to serve a Judean king. They want to negotiate easier conditions. Skeptical of the outcome, they contacted Jeroboam (a refugee in Egypt) to come. Under Solomon's rule, Jeroboam had been a mighty man of valor and industrious. He was previously over the labor force of the very prominent house of Joseph (1 Kings 11:28). He evidently gained a great reputation among them. He was a voice they could understand, and they wanted him there with them. Rather than sympathizing with the people's condition, Rehoboam took three days to consult with his advisers only to reject the wisdom of the older counselors who served Solomon and being persuaded by the harsh advice of young men. These men were Rehoboam's age; they grew up with him. He also ignored his father's proverb, "A soft answer turns away wrath, But a harsh word stirs up anger" (Proverbs 15:1). He spoke roughly, telling the people that his little finger would be thicker than his father's waist and that where his father chastised them with whips, he would chastise them with scourges—literally, scorpions (12:10-11, 14).

> But he **rejected** the advice which the **elders** had given him, and consulted the **young men** who had grown up with him, who stood before him.
>
> - 1 Kings 12:8

LESSON 5 Walking With Rehoboam and Jeroboam: A Kingdom Divides

Well, the people rebelled and stoned Adoram, his tax revenue officer, and even Rehoboam had to flee. After this, the people made Jeroboam king.

- Rehoboam didn't have the wisdom to see the signs of his time.
- Rehoboam didn't have the wisdom to recognize and lighten the people's burden.
- Rehoboam didn't have the heart of a servant.

Fill in the blanks

1 Kings 12:7
"And they spoke to him, saying, 'If you will be a _____ to these people today, and _____ them, and answer them, and speak good words to them, then they will be your _____ forever.'"

Questions

1. Have you been inclined to listen to the advice of the youth over the advice of your parents? Does that seem wise? _____

2. Why do you suppose that generally, the advice from parents and older people can be better than peers? _____

3. Who should have Rehoboam inquired of to get wisdom (Proverbs 2:6)? _____

4. List the action words that are needed for one to gain a heart of wisdom from Proverbs 2:1–5. _____

After the people rebelled, Rehoboam gathered an army of one hundred and eighty thousand warriors to defeat Israel and restore the kingdom. However, the Lord told him through the prophet Shemaiah to cease. Rehoboam obeyed (1 Kings 12:24). For the next four years, Rehoboam had reigned wisely strengthening his cities and building fortified strongholds. Every city had readymade weapons of shields and spears (2 Chronicles 11:11-12). However, when Rehoboam became militarily strong, he became spiritually weak and forsook God's law. God showed him how weak he really was by having Shishak, the king of Egypt invade his nation with twelve hundred chariots, sixty thousand horsemen, and an army without number (2 Chronicles 12:1-3). Shishak was ready and able to destroy Jerusalem, but the people humbled themselves and God granted Judah partial deliverance. They were not destroyed but the gold was taken away (2 Chronicles 12:9). The golden age had ended!

A likable but dangerous leader (1 Kings 12:25-33)

Reigning in Israel, King Jeroboam used his influence to lead the ten tribes of Israel into full religious apostasy from which they would never recover. Jeroboam's departure began a long journey of ungodly kings for the Northern Kingdom which ended in Assyrian domination. It also set in motion rapid doom upon Jeroboam's house—whoever belongs to him. Read 1 Kings 14:10-11.

Fill in the blanks

"The _____ shall eat whoever _____ to _____ and dies in the _____, and the _____ of the air shall eat whoever dies in the _____; for the LORD has spoken!"

- Jeroboam built up Shechem, the city in which he was made king, as the capital (1 Kings 12:25).

- Jeroboam feared that the people would be drawn back to the worship at Jerusalem and to King Rehoboam (1 Kings 12:26-27).

- Jeroboam received godless counsel and created his own religion which imitated Jerusalem's worship (1 Kings 12:28-33).

  - He made calves of gold. He wanted a sensory religion that could compete with Solomon's golden temple. He set these up at Bethel which was only about 12 miles north of Jerusalem and the other he set up at Dan. Remember Exodus 32:1-6.

  - He made shrines on the high places. God had chosen Jerusalem to be the place for worship (Deuteronomy 12:5-11; 1 Kings 11:36). These shrines were temples that he built to compete with the temple in Jerusalem.

  - He made priests from every class of people to serve at these shrines. God had chosen the Levites to serve in such a role (Numbers 1:50; 18:6; Deuteronomy 12:19; etc.). Jeroboam, however, believed he could relax these restrictions and replace them with people of his choice. Any man-made religion sets aside God's law and replaces it with a human will.

LESSON 5 Walking With Rehoboam and Jeroboam: A Kingdom Divides

- He created and substituted his own kind of feast on the fifteenth day of the eighth month. This feast served as a copycat of the Feast of Tabernacles, which was to be observed in Jerusalem on the fifteenth day of the seventh month (Leviticus 23:34).
- He sacrificed to the golden calves at Bethel. Jeroboam was very religious, and yet he was very wrong. Being religious does not make one right. For religion to be pure, it must faithfully serve the Lord and not substitute human ideas for God's commands.

Applications and study questions

Jeroboam changed the object of worship from God to golden calves. He changed the place of worship from Jerusalem to the various shrines he built. He changed the priesthood from Levites only, to those from any class. He changed the times of worship from the seventh month to the eighth month.

5. Who and how are we supposed to worship God (John 4:24)? _____
   _____
   _____

6. Do people try to change the church today from being "of Christ" to something else? In what way? _____
   _____
   _____
   _____

7. Do people change the object of our worship today to something else? Can you think of an example? _____
   _____
   _____
   _____

8. Do people change the times of certain acts of worship today to some other time? When are we supposed to gather as a church to give of our means and partake of the Lord's Supper (Acts 20:7; 1 Corinthians 16:1-2)? What if we were to do this on the seventh day of the week?_____
   _____
   _____
   _____
   _____

9. Do people change the leadership today from the kind that God has defined? _____

10. What kind of leadership has God defined and what would violate such?
    _____
    _____
    _____

    a. What kind of person does God want to serve as a preacher (2 Timothy 2:2; 4:2)? What would be a violation of this leadership role (1 Corinthians 14:34-35; 1 Timothy 2:12)? _____
       _____
       _____
       _____

    b. What kind of person does God want to serve as an overseer in the church (1 Timothy 3:1-7; Titus 1:5-9)? What kind of person would violate this leadership role and be banned from serving as such? Name as many examples as you can. _____
       _____
       _____
       _____
       _____
       _____

The Lesson of Deception—Two Prophets (1 Kings 13)

God sent a prophet to cry against the altar at Bethel (1 Kings 13:1-3). The altar split apart whereby Jeroboam charged the prophet to be arrested. However, God punished Jeroboam by having his hand wither. Unable to pull his hand back, Jeroboam pleaded for the prophet to pray for him to have his hand restored. Impressed with the healing, Jeroboam asked the prophet to come to his house, but the prophet refused his invitation because God had told him not to eat bread or drink water in this place as well as to return home taking a different way (1 Kings 13:8-9).

Upon hearing of this, an older prophet pursued the man of God and invited him to come to his home and eat. He lied to the younger prophet saying that God had changed his mind. The young prophet listened, left what he had known to be true, and blindly followed this unverifiable lie. After he ate, he was judged by the Lord for his disobedience and a lion came upon him and killed him (1 Kings 13:20-25).

LESSON 5 Walking With Rehoboam and Jeroboam: A Kingdom Divides

God made an example of the young prophet with a very important lesson attached to it. The lesson: While God may change his plans based on man's change of heart, He never changes His commandments. Any prophet that would say God's commandments have changed was to be marked a false prophet. Jeroboam had made like changes to God's law. He failed to learn from God's judgment against the man of God and continued in his sin. He secured the violent destruction of his house (1 Kings 13:33-34; 14:8-12). His son, Abijah became sick and died. His other son, Nadab, only reigned two years and was murdered through a conspiracy of a man named Baasha. Baasha also killed every person of Jeroboam's house; he did not leave even one alive (1 Kings 15:29). Jeroboam's sin not only affected him but his whole house as well as the nation of Israel. His house became dust in the wind. Proverbs 11:29, "He who troubles his own house will inherit the wind."

> And it was so, when he became king, that he **killed** all the house of **Jeroboam**. He did not leave to Jeroboam **anyone** that breathed, until he had **destroyed** him...
>
> - 1 Kings 15:29

True or false

11. **T or F** Rehoboam listened to the advice of older people.

12. **T or F** Jeroboam sought to restore the Law of God in the hearts of Israel.

13. **T or F** The king of Egypt took away a lot of gold from Judah during Rehoboam's reign.

14. **T or F** God punished a true prophet for his departure from a commandment to not eat bread in Israel.

15. **T or F** God would not punish Jeroboam for his false gods, false feast, and false priesthood in Bethel.

16. **T or F** Jeroboam heeded the example of the prophet who was killed by a lion and repented of his sins.

People of faith (2 Chronicles 11:13-17)

These Levites gave us a great example of what it means to seek first the kingdom of God (Matthew 6:33). They were able to look past the popularity of Jeroboam and the harshness of Rehoboam. They took a stand against Jeroboam's new religion and even left their common lands to move to travel to Jerusalem in order to faithfully serve God. Serving God will always have a cost. But not serving God will have a cost also. These priests were willing to lose their common lands but were walking toward God's promises. On the other hand, Jeroboam gained a lot of physical power, but was rejected by God and lost the enduring promises made to him.

Conclusion

We can see the folly of lacking wisdom and its damaging effects in Rehoboam's decision making. In the religious departure of Jeroboam, we can also view the folly of adding to God's word (Proverbs 30:5-6). In either case, sin is very destructive!

Walking With Jehoshaphat: The Danger of Evil Companionship

It has been about sixty years since the death of Solomon. In the year 870 BC, I became king at thirty-five years old. My mother's name is Azubah (2 Chronicles 20:31). My father, Asa, was a mighty king but suffered a severe malady in his feet and died in the forty-first year of his reign. Relying on the Lord, Asa and his military defeated an army of one million troops with 300 chariots commanded by Zerah, an Ethiopian (2 Chronicles 14:9)!

A prophet named Azariah, the son of Oded was a powerful messenger who heavily influenced my father to obey the Lord (2 Chronicles 15:1-7). He was clear in his message that if we seek God, He will be found, but if we forsake Him, He will forsake us. He commanded us to be strong and not weak and that our work would be rewarded!

My father was deeply moved by Azariah. He took courage and removed the abominable idols from the land of Judah and Benjamin. He also restored the altar of the Lord. He began a great return to true worship by seeking the Lord with all his heart. In the fifteenth year of his reign, great numbers of people came to Jerusalem, even from areas of Ephraim, Manasseh, and Simeon. Seven hundred bulls and seven thousand sheep were offered (2 Chronicles 15:8-11). The people entered into a covenant to seek the Lord with wholehearted fervor; it became a capital offense to not seek the Lord, whether male or female, small or great (2 Chronicles 15:12-15).

My father even removed his own grandmother, Maachah, (the granddaughter of the infamous son of David, Absalom) from the powerful position of "queen mother." She had made an obscene image

KEY PASSAGE

And he went out to meet Asa, and said to him: "Hear me, Asa, and all Judah and Benjamin. The LORD is **with you** while you are **with Him**. If you **seek** Him, He will be **found** by you; but if you forsake **Him**, He will forsake **you**."

- 2 Chronicles 15:2

of a false goddess, Asherah. Asa's devotion to God was stronger than his allegiance to family. He took her image and crushed it (2 Chronicles 15:16-17; see also 11:21; 1 Kings 15:10).

My father also strove to remove the high places in the cities of Judah but had not removed the high places of worship from the cities he occupied in Israel (2 Chronicles 14:3, 5; 15:17). When I became king, I also opposed these sinful places of pagan worship (2 Chronicles 17:6; 20:33). Unfortunately, the people would often have a divided heart and secretly build these places for idol worship. Such unfaithful worship would be the cause of destruction to our people (2 Kings 17:9).

Sadly, the warning Azariah: "The LORD is with you while you are with Him. If you seek Him, He will be found by you; but if you forsake Him, He will forsake you," fell on many deaf ears.

During my father's reign in Judah, the northern kingdom of Israel had great political unrest. Kings were being assassinated by others who wanted the throne (see 1 Kings 15:27; 16:9-10). Eventually, a powerful man named Omri became king of Israel in the twenty-seventh year of Asa's reign. After Omri won the crown of Israel, he later subdued Moab. He became so powerful that his name is found outside of the land of Israel! When Omri died, his son Ahab became king during my father's thirty-eighth year (1 Kings 16:29). Without knowing the consequences of unholy alliances, I became friends with Ahab. Therefore, the wisdom and warning of Solomon, my ancestor, has proven valid in my life's story. I am Jehoshaphat, the son of Asa, the son of Abijah, the son of Rehoboam, the son of Solomon, the son of David. I am the seventh king of Judah. *Come walk with me in my history.*

Inscription: "Omri had taken possession of the whole land of Medeba…"

(This photo by unknown author is licensed under CC BY-SA)

Fill in the blanks

Proverbs 12:26
"The _____ should _____ his _____ _____, For the way of the wicked leads them _____."

LESSON 6 Walking With Jehoshaphat: The Danger of Evil Companionship   47

Questions

1. In your own words, describe Azariah's message to Jehoshaphat's father (2 Chronicles 15:1-7).

   _____
   _____
   _____
   _____
   _____
   _____

2. How should a person seek the Lord and what would this require of a person (see Deuteronomy 4:29; Matthew 6:33)? _____
   _____
   _____
   _____

3. Asa received Azariah's preaching. Do you think Jehoshaphat would also heed his message?
   _____

> But **seek first** the kingdom of **God** and His **righteousness**, and **all** these things shall be **added** to you.
>
> - Matthew 6:33

The character of Jehoshaphat

Read 2 Chronicles 17:1-9. We find in Jehoshaphat a desire to obey what Azariah told Asa. Here is a list of some of the positive qualities of this king:

- He walked in the former ways of David (17:3). David was a man after God's heart. Jehoshaphat was too.
- He rejected the Baals (17:3). Baal was considered the chief male god; Ashtoreth was the chief goddess. After Israel came into the promised land, they developed a strong but fatal attraction to Baal worship (Judges 2:11-13; 3:7; etc.). Ahab had married Jezebel, a Baal worshiper. He built a temple for Baal in the capital city of Samaria (1 Kings 16:32). Baal means "lord" and is often

in the plural because each locality had its own Baal. He was a fertility and storm god. The worship of Baal appealed to sensuality perhaps in a similar way that much of what is passed off or promoted as entertainment does today.

- He sought the God of his father. What Azariah preached is what Jehoshaphat pursued.

- He walked in God's commandments rather than the acts of Israel.

- He commissioned men to teach the Law of the Lord in all the cities of Judah. One cannot walk with God, apart from the revealed will of God.

The success of Jehoshaphat

Read 2 Chronicles 17:10-19.

Because the king emphasized the law of the Lord, the fear of the Lord fell on all the surrounding kingdoms and God increasingly blessed him. Jehoshaphat became so respected that even Philistines and Arabians brought presents to him. He built fortresses, owned much property, and had a very large military consisting of 1,160,000 men of valor. He had riches and honor in abundance!

Jehoshaphat put his faith into practice. When he was being invaded by a great company of enemy soldiers, he inquired of the Lord, heeded the voice of God and commanded his army to trust in God. He was delivered by God who set confusion among the enemy. These events are recorded in 2 Chronicles 20:1-30.

The pitfall for Jehoshaphat (2 Chronicles 18:1-3)

The real danger to Jehoshaphat was not an enemy army invading him. When that happened, God destroyed the enemy. Pride was not his pitfall. He remained humble all his life. His faith did not unravel by unbelief. He never stopped believing in God and frequently taught others to fully trust in

> Do not **enter** the path of the **wicked**, And do not **walk** in the way of **evil**.
> - Proverbs 4:14

LESSON 6 Walking With Jehoshaphat: The Danger of Evil Companionship

Jehovah. The dangerous trap was evil companionships. Solomon's warning to not set your foot on the pathway of wicked men was ignored (Proverbs 1:15; 4:14).

By marriage, Jehoshaphat allied himself with one of the evilest persons of all—Ahab. Ahab threw a very large and generous feast for Jehoshaphat and those who were with him. Ahab appeared hospitable by killing sheep and oxen in abundance for Jehoshaphat's arrival. On this occasion, Ahab persuaded Jehoshaphat to join him in war against a common foe.

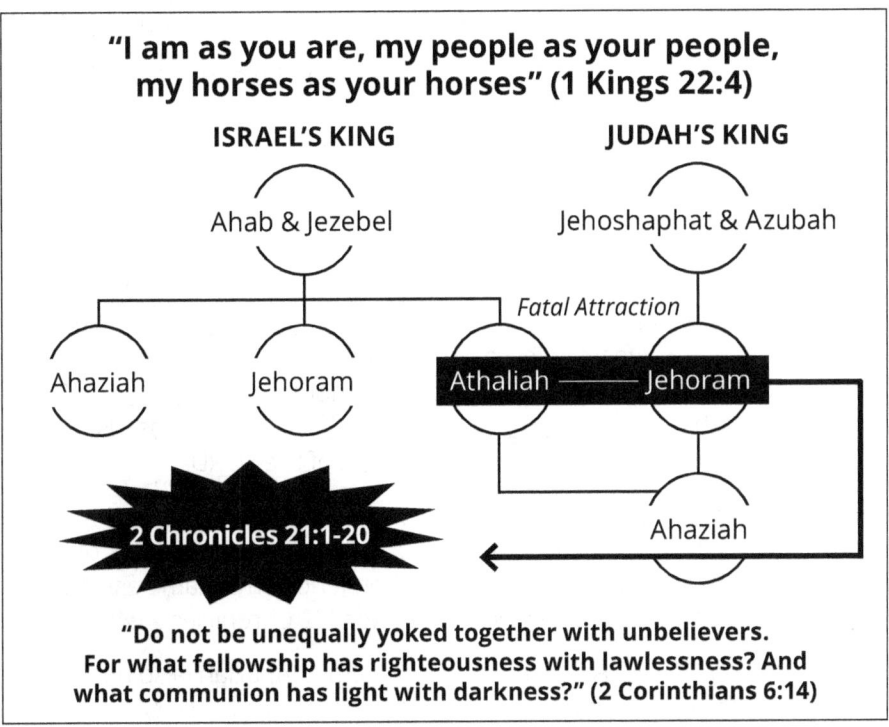

This alliance proved dangerous to Jehoshaphat's own life. The Syrians had taken Ramoth Gilead from Israel's control and Ahab wanted it back. Going against popular opinion, the prophet Micaiah told Ahab he would perish if he went to war (2 Chronicles 18:1-17). Yet Ahab refused to listen to the prophet disguising himself in the war to not look like the king, he convinced Jehoshaphat to wear royal garments, perhaps as a decoy. As Ahab planned, the Syrians mistook Jehoshaphat as Ahab and pursued him. Unlike Ahab, Jehoshaphat cried out to the Lord and God delivered him. As the battle continued, an archer's arrow pierced through Ahab's armor mortally wounding him. As Micaiah had warned so Ahab died. Jehoshaphat nearly died. Was it worth it for Jehoshaphat to ally himself with Ahab? When Jehoshaphat returned to Jerusalem, Jehu, the son of a seer rebuked him.

Fill in the blanks

2 Chronicles 19:2
"And Jehu the son of Hanani the seer went out to meet him, and said to King Jehoshaphat, 'Should you _____ the _____ and _____ those who _____ the LORD? Therefore the wrath of the LORD is upon you.'"

Darkness further invaded Jehoshaphat's house when his son, Jehoram, married Athaliah, Ahab's daughter. Athaliah became a scourge spiritually, physically, and royally, not only to Jehoshaphat's house but to all of Judah.

Spiritually: She brought the idolatrous influence of the house of Ahab with her. She influenced Jehoshaphat's son, Jehoram, and grandson, Ahaziah to behave very wickedly. Elijah had sent a letter condemning him and judging him for his wayward and idolatrous deeds (2 Chronicles 21:12-15).

Fill in the blanks

1 Kings 8:17-18
"He was thirty-two years old when he became _____, and he reigned _____ years in Jerusalem. And he _____ in the way of the kings of _____, just as the house of _____ had done, for the _____ of _____ was his _____; and he did evil in the sight of the LORD."

Physically: After Jehoshaphat died, his own son Jehoram nearly extinguished Jehoshaphat's dynasty because he conducted his life like the kings of Israel rather than his father and grandfather. When Jehoram became established as king, he killed all his brothers with the sword (2 Chronicles 21:4).

Royally: Jehoram's wife, Athaliah, had a son named Ahaziah (also named Jehoahaz). Athaliah counseled him with ungodly advice to live wickedly (2 Chronicles 22:3). Ahaziah only reigned one year when he was caught in Samaria and put to death by Jehu, one who became king over Israel and a destroyer of the house of Ahab. When Athaliah (Ahab's daughter) found out that her son was killed, she went on a rampage to murder all the potential royal heirs to the throne and then she reigned over the land for six years (2 Chronicles 22:10-12).

From an unholy alliance between Jehoshaphat and Ahab came a succession of events that led to the near extermination of the entire lineage of Jehoshaphat! Yet, by the providence of God and through the brave efforts of Jehoshabeath, the daughter of Jehoram and sister of Ahaziah, the last remaining heir was saved! Jehoshabeath (also named, Jehosheba in 2 Kings 11:2) stole the child Joash away and hid him from Athaliah for six years until he could become king.

Jehoshaphat: The Danger of Evil Companionship

Complete the crossword puzzle below.

Across

4. The Moabite Stone mentions this king of Israel
5. The prophet of the Lord who Ahab said hated him
7. The son of Asa
8. The granddaughter of Absalom and grandmother of Asa
9. The son of Omri
11. The father of Jehoshaphat
13. How should the righteous choose friends? See Proverbs 12:26
15. The son of Jehoram who became king
16. The chief male god of Canaan

Down

1. Commanded one million troops and three hundred chariots
2. The great-grandfather of Asa
3. The mother of Jehoshaphat
6. The son of Oded and prophet who influenced Asa
7. The daughter of Jehoram who hid Joash from Athaliah
10. The daughter of Ahab and wife of Jehoram
12. The wife of Ahab
14. A son of Ahab that shares the same name as the son of Jehoshaphat (2 Kings 3:1)

Created using the Crossword Maker on TheTeachersCorner.net

Conclusion

The life of Jehoshaphat teaches us the great importance associated with who we pick as friends as well as who we choose to marry. Not only can these people influence us here; they also can have an influence on our children and even grandchildren in the time to come.

1 Corinthians 15:33: "Do not be deceived: 'Evil company corrupts good habits.'"

Lesson 7
Walking With Elijah: The Challenger of False Religion

The land of Israel is filled with altars of sin. Solomon introduced false religions during his reign. Jeroboam went a further step in building golden calves of worship to replace the true worship of Jerusalem. Ahab went beyond the sins of Jeroboam and built an actual temple to the false god, Baal. Baal worship robs the true and living God of His glory and appeals to man's sensual desires to make him altogether corrupt.

With as much fervor as I oppose everything about this fake god and his religion, the king of Israel and his wife Jezebel promote it with equal enthusiasm. To be a prophet of Baal proves to be financially rewarding. However, to stand with Jehovah proves to be hazardous at best. Several prophets of God have already been massacred by Jezebel while the false prophets of Baal eat at Jezebel's table. The people of the land are caught up in the dilemma and have not decided whether Baal or Jehovah is the true Lord of the earth.

As Moses, the servant of God called down the plagues against the false Egyptian deities of his day, so I have called upon heaven to restrain any rain (including the dew) from falling on Israel to show the utter weakness of the so-called god, Baal. People reverence Baal as a storm god. I will show them who the true God of fire, rain, and life is.

I am Elijah the Tishbite. Jehovah is my God, which is my name's meaning and what I believe. *Come walk with me in my history!*

Ahab, the troubler of Israel (1 Kings 16:25-34)

There are hard times for the faithful in Israel. Ahab assumed the throne of his father Omri

KEY PASSAGE

Elijah was a man with a **nature** like **ours**, and he **prayed earnestly** that it would not **rain**; and it **did not rain** on the land for **three years and six months**.

- James 5:17

in the thirty-eighth year of Asa. As of this text, there have been seven transitions of kings in Israel to only three in Judah! Political instability is one of the characteristics of the northern kingdom. Unfaithfulness is the key characteristic of the northern kingdom.

Sin pathway progresses downward. Ahab did more evil in the sight of the Lord than all who were before him. The sins of Jeroboam which brought on the extermination of Jeroboam's house was considered trivial to Ahab. This led to choosing to marry a foreigner from Sidon and a Baal worshiper—Jezebel. This woman was a very bad choice for him.

Fill in the blanks

1 Kings 21:25
"But there was no one like Ahab who _____ himself to do _____ in the sight of the LORD, because _____ his _____ _____ him up."

Traveling on the pathway of sin also led Ahab to fully embrace Baal worship. He "served" and "worshiped" him (1 Kings 16:32). This led further to the construction of an altar and temple for Baal which he built in the capital city of Samaria. Ahab also made a wooden image. He, therefore, broke the first two commands of the covenant he was under:

- You shall have no other gods before me (Exodus 20:3).
- You shall not make for yourselves a carved image nor bow down to them and serve them (Exodus 20:4-5).

We will see in Ahab's life that his willingness to break the first two commandments made it easy to break many others.

Questions

1. What happened during the reign of Ahab in 1 Kings 16:34? What lesson can we learn from this text? _____
   _____
   _____
   _____

2. After Elijah returns in 1 Kings 18:17-18, Ahab greets Elijah calling him the troubler of Israel. Who does Elijah identify as the real troubler of Israel? What two reasons did Elijah give as the source of trouble? _____
   _____
   _____
   _____

Jehovah: the God of life
(1 Kings 17:1-24)

Hard times make for strong men. Elijah comes on the scene in all boldness. His message is clear, "As the Lord God of Israel lives" (17:1). Baal would be exposed to be less than a weak god, an unliving creation of man. To prove that Jehovah rules, Elijah prayed there would be no dew or rain these years except at his word. This took tremendous faith in Elijah's heart. During this time, everyone was looking for water and food. God provided both water and food to Elijah and Elijah would, through the power of God, provide water and food for the people. God commanded Elijah to go and hide by the brook Cherith which flows into the Jordan so that he could drink water. Meanwhile, God commanded the ravens to provide food for him in the morning and evening. God used birds to sustain Elijah with daily bread and meat. Being a drought, the brook eventually dried up. God's word again came to Elijah commanding him to go to the country of Sidon and dwell there. God commanded, of all people, a widow to provide for him. Many times God uses the weak and base things of the world to accomplish His will.

When Elijah enters the city of Zarephath he found the widow gathering sticks and requested a drink and a morsel of bread. She explained how she had nothing but a little flour and oil left to make them some food to eat, then die. She literally had nothing else. Yet Elijah told her to make him a cake first and to not fear for the flour shall not be used up nor shall the jar of oil run dry until the rain comes from the Lord. She believed him and did what he told her. Here is a case of a Gentile with great faith. Yet, most of Israel cannot determine if Jehovah or Baal is the true God of the earth. The Lord also implies that she received Elijah better than those in Israel would (cf. Luke 4:24-26).

Her faith was tested again for her son became sick unto death. She perceived that Elijah was visiting

> As the **Lord God** of Israel **lives**, before whom I stand, there shall not be **dew** nor **rain** these years, except at my **word**.
>
> - 1 Kings 17:1

judgment upon her for a secret sin which had now resurfaced in her mind. It is often in times of sorrow and tragedy that we can be moved to reflect on our soul's condition. She thought her sins were somehow deserving the death of her son. Yet Elijah took the child up to his room where he was staying, stretched out over the child three times and prayed for his soul to be restored. God answered his prayer and he presented him alive to his mother. The chapter begins with the affirmation that Jehovah is alive (17:1). At its end, we find that Jehovah is the God of life as Elijah said, "See, your son lives!" (17:23).

Questions

3. God used ravens to feed Elijah bread and meat. Can you think of other times where God used animals to get his will done or teach man lessons? _____
_____
_____

4. It was a miracle that the flour and oil never ran out. How many people did Jesus feed with only five barley loaves and two small fish (John 6:9)?
_____

5. God also gives us our daily bread. Do you thank Him daily for your meals? _____

Jehovah: the God of fire (1 Kings 18:20-46)

In the third year of the drought, God told Elijah to depart from the widow and present himself before Ahab (1 Kings 18:1). The famine was severe. Jezebel hunted down and had the prophets of Jehovah executed. We read of a righteous man named Obadiah who worked for Ahab. He was commissioned to find water and grass for the horses and mules. Instead, he found Elijah. Elijah told him to get Ahab. When they met, Ahab called Elijah the troubler of Israel. Elijah retorted that Ahab and his unfaithful house was what troubled Israel and that he needed to summon all Israel along with the prophets of Baal and Asherah to Mount Carmel (1 Kings 18:17-19). This was an army of false prophets that numbered eight hundred and fifty in sum.

When they were all gathered to Mount Carmel, Elijah forced the people to reach one of two conclusions.

LESSON 7 Walking With Elijah: The Challenger of False Religion

Fill in the blanks

1 Kings 18:21
"And _____ came to all the _____, and said, "How long will you falter between _____ _____? If the _____ is _____, follow Him; but if _____, follow him." But the people answered him not a _____."

The people answered him not a word. They were undecided as to who to follow. Their indecision was going to be short lived at this point. Elijah took a stand against the 850 false prophets and gave them a challenge. Take two bulls and they could choose one, Elijah would take the other. Slaughter the bull and place the meat on wood but use no fire. Elijah would do the same with the second bull. They will call on the name of their gods and Elijah will call on the name of Jehovah. Whoever answers by fire, He is God (18:24)!

All the people saw the challenge well and good. The prophets of Baal were to go first since they were many. They cut the bull in pieces, laid it on wood and cried out to Baal to hear them from morning until evening. There was no answer. They leaped around the altar...no answer. They cut themselves to where blood was gushing out of them, still, no answer. Elijah mocked them suggesting their god was meditating, too busy, on a journey, or perhaps was even sleeping! Regardless, the multitude of worshipers could not get an answer (1 Kings 18:26-29).

Elijah summoned all the people. He "repaired the altar of the Lord that was broken down" (1 Kings 18:30). He took twelve stones which corresponded to the number of tribes. Israel should have been united in the worship of Jehovah! He dug a trench around the altar. He put the wood in order and placed the butchered bull on top of the wood. He commanded to take four pots of water and pour it on the bull and wood. He told them to do it again

> For our **God** is a **consuming fire**.
>
> - Hebrews 12:29

a second and third time to where the trench was filled with water. After which, Elijah came near the altar at the time of the evening sacrifice, prayed to God to let it be known that He was God in Israel and that Elijah was His prophet and acted from the very word of God. As soon as Elijah ended his prayer the answer from God fell like an anvil dropping from the clouds. The fire of the Lord consumed the wood, the stones, the dust and licked up the water that was in the trench (1 Kings 18:38)!

The people were undecided no longer. They had a change of mind, from indecision to falling on their faces proclaiming that Jehovah is God! They had a change of affection. No longer were they clinging to Baal, but to the Lord. They had a change in action. They obeyed the prophet, seized the false prophets and executed them.

Not only is Jehovah the God of life (1 Kings 17); but he is the God of fire (1 Kings 18:38; Hebrews 12:29).

True or false

6. **T or F** Elijah's name means "Jehovah is my God."
7. **T or F** Elijah was the troubler of Israel.
8. **T or F** Elijah stood alone, confronting and mocking 850 false prophets.
9. **T or F** Jehovah is the only real and living God.
10. **T or F** Ahab was a righteous king.
11. **T or F** Ahab's wife was a godly, Hebrew woman.
12. **T or F** Ahab was more righteous than the other kings before him.
13. **T or F** Baal was a real god who at one time could control the weather.

Jehovah: the God of rain (1 Kings 18:41-46)

After the false prophets were executed, the drought was going to end with torrential rain. When there were no clouds to be seen, Elijah told Ahab there was the sound of abundant rain. It began with a cloud as small as a man's hand where the sun-filled sky quickly washed away into ominous, black clouds and blustery wind. Jehovah is the real storm-God!

Jesus said, "He makes His sun rise on the evil and on the good and sends rain on the just and on the unjust" (Matthew 5:45).

LESSON 7 Walking With Elijah: The Challenger of False Religion

What made Elijah great?

Elijah is one of the greatest prophets ever although he has no book in the Bible that bears his name. What made him so effective?

- Elijah was a man of prayer. He had earnest prayer (James 5:17). The Lord heard the voice of Elijah (1 Kings 17:22).

- Elijah was a truth-teller. He accurately spoke the word of the Lord. Notice, "Thus says the Lord God of Israel" (1 Kings 17:14). The widow knew that he spoke the word of the Lord (1 Kings 17:24).

- Elijah was willing to confront error. Where many run from confrontation, Elijah met it with the word of the Lord. In 1 Kings 21:1-16, Ahab coveted his neighbor's vineyard and agreed to a wicked plan to murder Naboth so as to steal his vineyard. Since Ahab broke the first two commandments that dealt with reverence toward God, he could easily break the other commandments which applied to his neighbor. God sent the prophet to rebuke Ahab's sin, 1 Kings 21:19, "You shall speak to him, saying, 'Thus says the LORD: "Have you murdered and also taken possession?"'" His message was direct and pointed.

- Elijah brought peace. He was not the troubler of Israel, Ahab was (1 Kings 18:18-19). Sin is what troubles God's people, not telling the truth.

Questions

14. Who must we please when we speak (1 Thessalonians 2:4)? _____

15. Ahab had been around several great prophets in his day, yet he refused to listen to their message. Why do you suppose people don't listen to the preaching of God's word today? _____
   _____
   _____
   _____

Conclusion

We can gain many lessons about the God we serve and the kind of people we should be when we walk with Elijah. There is more to be told, that can be read in the first two chapters of 2 Kings. Eventually, Elijah was taken up into the heavens in a chariot of fire. He had to deal with fear and discouragement, as we all do, yet he was not neutral against the forces of evil but challenged them. He then was rewarded for his faithfulness. Eventually, he would return to this world with Moses, standing with Jesus on a high mountain and conversing about the Lord's upcoming death (Luke 9:30-31).

Lesson 8
Walking With Elisha: Possessing a Double Spirit

My nation continues to be unfaithful to the Lord. Before I became a prophet, I was a farmer in Abel Meholah. One day when I was plowing, a man approached me and threw his mantle upon me as he was walking by. It was Elijah, the rugged prophet of God and challenger of false religion, the one who prayed for no rain as a judgment against Israel's unfaithfulness where there was no moisture (even dew) for the span of three years. This is he who was fed by ravens in the wilderness, raised a dead child to life again, defeated and had executed the prophets of Baal and did many mighty works in Israel.

Why was I chosen by Elijah? After the execution of the prophets of Baal, Elijah retreated from Jezreel to Beersheba having received a death notice from Jezebel, King Ahab's wife. He fled about 100 miles away. At Beersheba, he left his servant while he went a day's journey into the wilderness (1 Kings 19:3-4). Alone and depressed, Elijah asked God to take his life (1 Kings 19:5). However, an angel of the Lord provided him a cake with a jar of water and told him to arise and eat. Elijah was sent on a long journey deep into the wilderness. "His destination?" you ask. He traveled all the way to the mountain of God where Moses once stood before the Lord God to receive the Law (1 Kings 19:5-8).

By a miracle, the cake and water sustained Elijah for forty days and nights. God showed Elijah that he was not alone. In fact, as bad as things were, seven thousand Israelites lived faithfully to the Lord, not worshiping Baal. Upon leaving Mount Horeb, Elijah was commissioned to anoint a man named Hazael as king over Syria. A commander called Jehu would also be anointed a king over Israel. I was chosen

KEY PASSAGE

And so it was, when they had crossed over, that Elijah said to Elisha, "**Ask!** What may I do for you, before I am **taken away** from you?" Elisha said, "Please let a **double portion** of your **spirit** be upon me."

- 2 Kings 2:9

to be the prophet to carry on Elijah's work. Although Elijah convinced his former servant to remain in Beersheba, I determined to never be persuaded to leave his side until his departure from this life comes.

During these troublesome times in Israel, Elijah became my mentor and friend. My request was simple? I wanted a double portion of his spirit. My name is Elisha. *Come walk with me in my history!*

Similarities

Elisha is first introduced in 1 Kings 19. His work as a minister of Elijah and prophet of God spans from Chapters 2-9 and 13 of 2 Kings. He performed more miracles than any other prophet in the Bible other than Moses. Like Elijah, Elisha has no book of the Bible bearing his name. Elijah means, "Jehovah is my God." Elisha means, "God is salvation." In the biblical account, they would both divide the waters of the Jordan, brought saving water, brought blessings to a widow, raised an only son back to life, dealt with unruly kings and summoned the wrath of God on unbelievers.

Burning his plow (1 Kings 19:19-21)

This text suggests that Elisha was the son of a man of wealth. A yoke is a wooden piece of equipment that binds two animals together to share a burden. Elisha had twelve pairs of these animals yoked together to plow.

A line drawing of a yoke of oxen.[1]

Likely his father's servants were busy plowing with the other eleven. While with the twelfth, Elijah came. God tested Elisha's character as to whether he was willing to wholeheartedly depart from his parents and material possessions to serve a prophet during this time of moral decline. Elisha passed the test. He ran after Elijah understanding what this duty required. He respectfully asked permission to bid his family farewell so that they would know why he left. He then took a yoke of oxen and slaughtered them, boiled their flesh using the wooden equipment, and gave it to the people to eat. He had fully and formally left his occupation as a farmer.

Then he arose and followed Elijah and became his servant. Elisha's journey to becoming the great prophet we read about today started with servitude. Similarly, in Luke 14:15-33, Jesus taught us that we must serve Him and love Him more than any job, any possession, or even any relationship that can be found on earth.

[1] "Yoke," by Pearson Scott Foresman. Source: https://commons.wikimedia.org/wiki/File:Yoke_(PSF).png#filelinks. Licensed under CC BY-SA.

LESSON 8 Walking With Elisha: Possessing a Double Spirit

Questions

1. What was Elisha doing when he was called to become God's prophet?
   _____
   _____

2. What was required of Elisha to become God's prophet? _____
   _____
   _____

3. What three excuses did Jesus show that men would give to excuse themselves from coming to Him (see Luke 14:15-20). _____
   _____
   _____
   _____

4. If you were Elisha, would you have burned your father's plow and sacrificed your oxen to follow Elijah? _____

5. Are there things in your life that you must burn in order to follow Christ? _____

The departure and blessing (2 Kings 2:1-15)

When Elijah's departure drew near, he told Elisha to stay and that he was going to Bethel. This is the place where Jacob saw the vision of the ladder with angels ascending and descending in Genesis 28:10-22. Sadly, Jeroboam turned this place into an altar for sin (1 Kings 12:28-29). Elisha displayed an earnest resolve to never leave Elijah.

Fill in the blanks

2 Kings 2:2
"Then Elijah said to Elisha, '_____ here, _____, for the LORD has sent me on to Bethel.' But Elisha said, 'As the LORD _____, and as your soul _____, I will _____ _____ _____!' So they went down to Bethel."

At Bethel, Elijah again told Elisha to stay as he traveled to Jericho. Elisha persisted with the same resolve. At Jericho headed toward the Jordan, Elijah asked a third time but Elisha remained steadfast still. After these three tests, Elijah asked Elisha what he could do for him. Elisha's response: "Please let a double portion of your spirit be upon me" (2 Kings 2:9). The request is like that of a firstborn who desires the double portion from the father (Deuteronomy 21:17). Elisha seems to deeply desire the double portion of Elijah's spirit to be viewed as a firstborn heir of Elijah's prophetic office and to carry on his work in Israel.

Elijah consented with a condition that Elisha must see Elijah's departure or not receive this blessing. As they continued and talked a dramatic scene unfolded. A chariot of fire appeared with horses of fire that separated the two. A whirlwind arose and carried Elijah up into heaven! As spectacular as this scene was, separation is always difficult and will always be sad when those we love depart from us. Elisha called out to Elijah, "My father, the chariot of Israel and its horsemen!" This seems to show that he viewed Elijah and his work as the strength of Israel, and in Elijah's departure, Israel's strength departed. This was similar to what King Joash would say about Elisha at his death (2 Kings 13:14).

Lessons

- We must recognize our departure is coming and be ready for it.
- Our resolve to follow Christ through Bethel or Jericho must be firm even until it takes us to the banks of the Jordan river (death). Only then can we receive the benefits of following the Lord (see Revelation 2:10).
- When death separates us from those we love and admire, the work of Christ must go on and there must be those in each generation willing to carry that work on.
- When God connects conditions to receive His blessings, we must fully comply with those conditions.

Blessings from God are conditional

Read the text and show what the problem is, what the condition is, and what blessing was gained.

> ...Be **faithful** until **death**, and I will give you the crown of **life**.
>
> - Revelation 2:10b

LESSON 8 Walking With Elisha: Possessing a Double Spirit 65

6. 2 Kings 3:19-22
   The problem: _____
   _____

   The solution with the conditions: _____
   _____
   _____

   The blessing: _____
   _____
   _____

7. 2 Kings 4:1-7
   The problem: _____
   _____

   The solution with the conditions: _____
   _____
   _____

   The blessing: _____
   _____
   _____

8. 2 Kings 4:38-41
   The problem: _____
   _____

   The solution with the conditions: _____
   _____
   _____

   The blessing: _____
   _____
   _____

9. 2 Kings 5:1-14
   The problem: _____
   _____

   The solution with the conditions: _____
   _____
   _____

   The blessing: _____
   _____
   _____

10. 2 Kings 6:1-7
    The problem: _____
    _____
    The solution: _____
    _____
    _____
    The blessing: _____
    _____
    _____

Questions

11. What is man's problem (Romans 3:23; 6:23)? _____
    _____

12. What conditions must a man do to receive the blessings of salvation (Mark 16:16; Acts 2:38; Romans 10:9-10)? _____
    _____
    _____

13. Can we ignore any of these conditions and expect God to save us? _____

Mocking, then mauled (2 Kings 2:23-25)

The prophets of God not only brought tidings of good things but also demonstrated the fiery judgment of God against evil.

When King Ahaziah was injured, he foolishly inquired of Baal-Zebub, the god of Ekron. For his error, God judged that he would not recover from his injury and would die in his bed. When the king learned that this was spoken through Elijah, he sent a captain of fifty men who went and demanded Elijah to come to the king (2 Kings 1:1-9). However, Elijah called down fire from heaven, and it consumed them all. This happened a second time and with the same result (2 Kings 1:10-12). A third company was sent to get Elijah, but the captain requested in humility for Elijah to come and begged him to consider his life as precious. Elijah went.

After Elijah's departure, Elisha went up to Bethel (the place of calf worship), where a gang of youths came out mocking him for his physical appearance. While Elijah was marked as being hairy, Elisha was bald (cf. 2 Kings 1:8). They likely recognized he was a prophet of Jehovah and went to make fun of him, calling him "baldhead." They did not have respect for Jehovah, His law, or His prophets. Elisha invoked divine vengeance upon these untrained, rude

LESSON 8 Walking With Elisha: Possessing a Double Spirit 67

youths, sending two female bears which mauled 42 of them! The Hebrew word and tense suggest a ripping or tearing up (translated "rip open" in 2 Kings 8:12 and "tear" in Ezekiel 13:11; Hosea 13:8). Bible commentator Matthew Henry pondered the following sobering thought:

> "And what will be the anguish of those parents, at the day of judgment, who witness the everlasting condemnation of their offspring, occasioned by their own bad example, carelessness, or wicked teaching!"[2]

These scenes should remind us of the duty to train children up in the fear of the Lord and the severity of being an enemy of God (Proverbs 22:6; Ecclesiastes 12:13; Romans 11:22).

Lessons

- The sins of one's youth can be very destructive.
- God hears the words we speak (see Matthew 12:36).
- The home's education and a person's associations can have a tremendous influence on the way young people behave.
- Parents who fail to walk children on the road of uprightness will become troubled by the predators on the pathway of wickedness. Tragically, it took 42 funerals to teach Bethel about reverence.

Questions

14. If you lived then, what would you have done?

    a. If you live in Bethel in Elisha's day, would you have participated with your peers or abstained? _____

    _____

> Therefore consider the **goodness** and **severity** of God: on those who **fell**, **severity**; but toward **you**, **goodness**, if you **continue** in His goodness. Otherwise you also will be **cut off**.
>
> - Romans 11:22

[2] 2 Kings 2, *Matthew Henry's Commentary.*
biblehub.com/commentaries/mhc/2_kings/2.htm.

b. Would you have sought the truth at Jerusalem or followed your family's faith that was conveniently practiced in Bethel? _____

15. Since you live now, what do you do?

    a. How do you view and treat those who teach God's word today?
    _____
    _____

    b. How do you view and treat those with physical disorders today?
    _____
    _____

    c. How do you view and treat those who are older than you today?
    _____
    _____

Conclusion

There is so much more we could say about the life of Elisha. In him, we find a model of spiritual strength. Elisha was hard working. He worked hard for his parents when he lived there in that he was in the field plowing (1 Kings 19:19). He worked hard for Elijah as his minister. He was committed. He refused to leave Elijah's side until he departed (2 Kings 2:6). He deeply respected Elijah and the office he held and therefore wanted a double portion of his spirit. When he spoke, he spoke by the authority of God: "Thus says the LORD" (2 Kings 3:16). He lived to maintain his honor (2 Kings 5:15-16). Sadly, his servant, Gehazi, was dishonest and covetous (2 Kings 5:20-27). Elisha put everything in all that he did and expected others to do the same. At his death, he told Joash, king of Israel, that he must strike the Syrians to destroy them (2 Kings 13:17). He then told Joash to take some arrows and strike the ground. Joash unenthusiastically struck the ground three times. This angered Elisha; he told him he should have struck five or six times, for then he would have struck Syria to destroy it (2 Kings 13:18-19).

Fill in the blanks

Ecclesiastes 9:10
"_____ your _____ finds to do, do it with your _____; for there is no work or device or knowledge or wisdom in the grave where you are going."

Lesson 9

Walking With King Jehu: Unfaithful Zeal

One day I was with some of the other captains of Israel's army in Ramoth Gilead, when something very strange happened that would make me become the eleventh king of Israel in 841 BC. It would involve great acts of violence and treason. Let me first introduce you to what led up to this day.

My commander, Bidkar, and I used to serve Ahab in his military campaigns. One day his neighbor's prime vineyard caught Ahab's eye and he wanted to buy it. Now, when Ahab and Jezebel really want something, they usually find a way to get it. For example, Jezebel loved the religion of Baal, so Ahab built a temple to promote Baal worship in Israel and even provided state support of such prophets (1 Kings 16:32). Who would ever have thought that in the area of the world near Solomon's golden temple in Judah, that Ahab would build a competing temple in honor of Baal? Perhaps Ahab thought he was to Baal as Solomon was to Jehovah. Like Solomon, Ahab built cities and where Solomon built a fabulous palace from cedars from Lebanon, Ahab built a palace of ivory (1 Kings 22:39)! Whatever Ahab and Jezebel want is what they get! If Jezebel despised Jehovah as the God of Israel, then she found a way to execute His prophets (1 Kings 18:4).

Unfortunately for Naboth. When he was unwilling to sell his vineyard, Jezebel worked out a plan to take it so her moping husband would smile again. She hired two false witnesses to testify in public that Naboth had blasphemed both God and the king. Shortly afterward, Naboth was stoned to death and Ahab arose to take possession of his prize (1 Kings 21:11-16). Even Naboth's sons, the rightful heirs, lost their lives in this take over (2 Kings 9:26). What Ahab wants is what Ahab gets, or so it seems.

KEY PASSAGE

Then he said, "Come with me, and see my **zeal** for the **LORD**." So they had him ride in his chariot.

- 2 Kings 10:16

Bidkar and I were riding with Ahab to Naboth's vineyard when all of a sudden, Elijah, the man of God, boldly approached and withstood Ahab to his face. Elijah pronounced a judgment of condemnation graphically detailing the total extermination of Ahab's house. He also spoke of Jezebel's disgraceful death where the dogs would consume her by the city's wall (1 Kings 21:17-24). I never forgot that day nor the boldness of the prophet withstanding such a powerful and dangerous king. Surprisingly, it brought Ahab to mourning, tearing his clothes, wearing sackcloth, and fasting. Consequently, his sentence was delayed until his sons ascended the throne (1 Kings 21:25-29).

After Ahab was mortally shot in battle at Ramoth Giliead, his son, Ahaziah, became king. His reign fell short! In his second year, Ahaziah literally fell from the upstairs through a lattice that landed him in a bed of affliction from which he would never recover. He soon died as the prophet Elijah said (2 Kings 1:4). A lattice worked like a window screen or trellis and would provide some privacy, allowing a cool breeze to enter the house while keeping out the sun's hot rays. Since Ahaziah had no son, his brother Joram (a nickname for Jehoram) ascended to the throne. Joram ruled for twelve years (as long as Omri, Ahab's father, reigned).

In Joram's twelfth year, a young man was sent by Elisha to find me in Ramoth Giliead. While I was sitting with some other captains, he said, "I have a message for you Commander." Those around me thought he was a madman. Not knowing who he was speaking to, I asked, "For which one of us?" and he responded, "For you, Commander." I followed him into a house and he anointed me with oil and proclaimed that I was chosen by Jehovah to be king over Israel (2 Kings 9:6). What he commissioned me to do was to become an avenger of all the blood Ahab's house was responsible for shedding in view of the prophets. I was to carry out the divine punishment long ago predicted. My reign is violent. My reign is bloody. The house that massacred the prophets will now be massacred. I pursued these orders with zeal at full throttle. I am Jehu. *Come **ride** with me in my history!*

Fill in the blanks

1 Kings 9:7-9
"You shall _____ down the _____ of _____ your _____, that I may _____ the _____ of My _____ the _____, and the blood of all the _____ of the LORD, at the hand of Jezebel. For the _____ _____ of _____ shall _____; and I will cut off from Ahab all the _____ in Israel, both bond and free. So I will make the _____ of Ahab like the house of _____ the son of Nebat, and like the house of _____ the son of Ahijah."

LESSON 9 Walking With King Jehu: Unfaithful Zeal

Baal worship had grown extensively in Israel during the reign of Ahab's house. His children were also wicked men. His wife stirred him up to do many wicked things. Jehu was anointed to bring on his house what had happened to Jeroboam's and Baasha's house.

The first objective: conspiring against the king (2 Kings 9:14-29). Abandoning the defense of Ramoth Giliead, Jehu went to the city of Jezreel, where King Joram was laid up due to the wounds he received in battle. Ahaziah (Joram's nephew and current king of Judah) was also there visiting.

A watchman saw Jehu's company approaching the palace at Jezreel. The king sent out horsemen to meet Jehu and see if all was well. However, rather than coming back to report to the king, they followed Jehu. Joram made his chariot ready and he went out with Ahaziah to meet Jehu on the property of Naboth and asked if Jehu's visit was of peace (2 Kings 9:22). Jehu responded, "What peace, as long as the harlotries of your mother Jezebel and her witchcraft are so many?" The two kings fled, but Jehu drew his bow "with full strength" and shot Jehoram between his arms and through his heart. They threw his body into the field of Naboth fulfilling the word of the Lord. Jehu pursued Ahaziah and they fatally shot him with an arrow and sent his body to be buried in Jerusalem. This would end any peace treaty between Israel and Judah. It would also cause chaos to erupt in Judah due to no one being capable to assume the throne. Athaliah, Ahaziah's mother went about destroying all the royal heirs to the throne and sought to rule herself (2 Chronicles 22:9; 2 Kings 11:1-3).

The second objective: destroying Jezebel, the queen mother (2 Kings 9:30-37). Jehu returned to Jezreel and found Jezebel who had heard of Jehu's deeds. She improved her appearance by painting her eyes and adorning her head (likely with royal apparel). This would prove of no benefit to her. She called out to Jehu claiming he was Zimri, a king who

> So the watchman reported, saying, "He went up to them and is **not coming back**; and the driving is like the driving of **Jehu** the son of Nimshi, for he **drives furiously**!"
>
> - 2 Kings 9:20

assassinated his king to only live seven days when Omri came and took the crown. Jehu called out, "Who is on my side?" Two or three eunuchs looked out to him with consent. He commanded that they throw the queen mother out of the window to the ground where he trampled her. He went inside the house to eat and when he came outside, he found that the dogs had eaten her corpse fulfilling 1 Kings 21:23.

The third objective: destroying the rest of Ahab's relatives (2 Kings 10:1-15). Jehu sent a letter to Samaria challenging them to set one of Ahab's sons on the throne and fight. However, they were afraid to declare a king and were willing to become Jehu's servants. Jehu then wrote them again telling them to prove their allegiance to him by beheading all of Ahab's sons. They slaughtered seventy. On the way to Samaria, he found some of Ahaziah's brethren and likewise put all 42 of them to death. When he came to Samaria, he destroyed all who remained to Ahab, fulfilling the word of the Lord spoken by Elijah.

The fourth objective: destroying all traces of Baal worship (2 Kings 10:16-28). Jehu worked deceptively in announcing his desire to offer a great sacrifice for Baal. He wanted every prophet, servant, and priest of Baal to be present. He sent throughout all Israel an invitation exclusively for all Baal worshipers to come to this sacrifice and proclaimed a solemn assembly. Every worshiper showed up and the temple of Baal was full. As soon as Jehu made an end to his offering, he commanded the guards and captains, "Go in and kill them; let no one come out!" (2 Kings 10:25). After they put them to death, they took out the sacred pillars of the temple and burned them, broke the temple down, and turned it into a dump. Jehu, therefore, defiled and utterly destroyed Baal from Israel.

True or false

1. **T or F** Ahab reigned 22 years (1 Kings 16:29).
2. **T or F** Israel's king, Joram, was Ahaziah's son.
3. **T or F** Judah's king, Ahaziah, was a nephew to King Joram.
4. **T or F** Jezebel tried to restrain Ahab's madness (1 Kings 21:25).
5. **T or F** Jehu was a king of peace.
6. **T or F** Jehu served Jehovah with a loyal heart like David.

Conclusion

Jehovah told Jehu that because he had done well in executing the house of Ahab, that he would have four generations reign as king in Israel (2 Kings 20:30). Jehu would reign for 28 years. His son, Jehoahaz, would reign for 17 years (2 Kings 13:1-9). His grandson, Jehoash (also named Joash) would reign 16 years and was with Elisha when he died (2 Kings 13:10-21). His great-grandson, Jeroboam, reigned for 41 years (2 Kings 14:23). His great-great-grandson, Zechariah, reigned for only six months. All of Jehu's descendants who reigned as king worked evil in the sight of the Lord.

Jehu could have set an example of not only opposing Baal but promoting the law of Jehovah. Sadly he did not turn away from the golden calves and lived with disregard toward the Law of Moses.

Fill in the blanks

2 Kings 10:31
"But Jehu took no heed to _____ in the _____ of the LORD God of Israel with _____ his _____; for he did not depart from the sins of Jeroboam, who had made Israel sin."

Jehu served Jehovah in destroying Ahab's house and Baal worship from a purely political motive. Although he had great zeal, he lacked the qualities of faithful zeal. He lacked humility and boasted of his own zeal toward the Lord (2 Kings 10:16). He lacked fervor against other things that were sinful. He continued in the sin of Jeroboam in the golden calves (2 Kings 10:29). He lacked wholehearted zeal for God's ways (2 Kings 10:31).

Although he reigned 28 years, nothing is written about that time other than God began to cut away parts of Israel from his control (2 Kings 10:32-36). There is preserved in archaeological artifacts a depiction of King Jehu in the "Black Obelisk." This four-sided pillar stands six feet, six inches high with five panels of pictures found on each side. It was found in the ancient Assyrian city of Calah by Henry Layard in November 1845.[1] It

"The Black Obelisk." A picture of side one, panel two of the Black Obelisk depicting Jehu bowing before the Assyrian king, Shalmaneser.[2]

depicts Jehu kissing the ground and offering tribute before the Assyrian king, Shalmaneser III. Deciphered, this stone seems to relate what Jehu did in 841 BC. While conspiring against his king, he was paying tribute to the Assyrians. This aspect of Jehu's reign was not related to the inspired writer's purpose, but archaeology provides us further historical insight into the acts of Jehu.

[1] Millard, Alan Ralph. *Treasures from Bible Times*. Lion, 1991. pp. 119–120.
[2] Steven G. Johnson (https://commons.wikimedia.org/wiki/File:Jehu-Obelisk-cropped.jpg), "Jehu-Obelisk-cropped", https://creativecommons.org/licenses/by-sa/3.0/legalcode

Questions

7. How must one love God to be accepted by Him (Deuteronomy 6:5-6)?
   _____

8. Jehu teaches us that doing something that is right with the wrong motive will not be acceptable to God. From the Scriptures below, what is approved? What canceled the good work?

   a. Acts 5:1-10
      Identify the good work: _____
      _____

      Identify what canceled the good work: _____
      _____

      Identify the consequence that followed: _____
      _____

   b. 1 Corinthians 13:1-4
      Identify the good work: _____
      _____

      Identify what canceled the good work: _____
      _____

      Identify the consequence that followed: _____
      _____

9. Zeal is required of us to be pleasing to God (Ecclesiastes 9:10; Romans 12:11; Revelation 3:19). From the Scriptures below, what must accompany zeal for one to be acceptable to God?

   a. Romans 10:2-3 _____
      _____

   b. 1 Corinthians 14:12 _____
      _____

   c. Galatians 4:18 _____
      _____

Lesson 10

Walking With King Hezekiah: Strengthened by God

People use an expression, "Like father, like son." Is this expression something that must always ring true? Would I be destined to imitate my father? I shuttered at that thought. Life is about choices... choices are channels that prove a person's character. While character is not inherited nor necessarily based on a single choice, the pattern of our decisions reveals and defines our character. Therefore, character is something developed by our will. I can choose my character! My wise ancestor, Solomon, penned that we can have help from God in making choices in building character. I can choose to know and bind mercy and truth around my neck and inscribe it in my heart to gain favor, unlike my father, who had disfavor with God and man. I could choose to not do what he did. I could also choose to do what he would not do. As Solomon wrote, I can lean on the Lord for understanding and He will direct me and guide me as a father (Proverbs 3:5-12).

I lived my life to contradict the "Like father, like son" idea. I openly rejected the sinful departures of our ancestors (2 Chronicles 29:6). Although my mother, Abi, was the daughter of Zechariah (2 Kings 18:2; 2 Chronicles 29:1; cf. 26:5), my father, Ahaz, chose to be wicked. He lived with all the wrong priorities. He disgraced our name and nation. When he died, we refused to bury him in the tombs of the kings (2 Chronicles 28:27). Ahaz chose to contradict the good example of my grandfather, Jotham. He chose to walk like the kings of Israel. He built molded images for the Baals, and among other crimes, he even burned one son in the fire as homage to his false gods (2 Kings 16:3). He deserved to be stoned (Leviticus 18:21; 20:2). He chose disgrace rather than honor.

KEY PASSAGE

Let not **mercy** and **truth** forsake you; **bind** them around your **neck**, **write** them on the tablet of your **heart**, and so find **favor** and high **esteem** in the sight of **God** and **man**.

- Proverbs 3:3-4

He searched for security in political measures rather than turning to the Lord. When Rezin, the king of Syria and Pekah, the king of Israel plotted to overthrow Judah, he didn't listen to the prophet Isaiah regarding these two (Isaiah 7:1-8). Rather, he sought comfort in working with the godless Assyrians. For him, leaning on the Lord was not an option. When Syria attacked our land and carried off a great multitude, Pekah also killed one hundred and twenty thousand mighty men of Judah in one day. If it were not for the prophet Oded and some of the heads of the children of Israel, Pekah would have enslaved two hundred thousand of our women, sons, and daughters (2 Chronicles 28:6-15). They were set free by the fear of God, not the help of Assyria. Ahaz sent silver and gold from the house of the Lord as a gift to the king Tiglath-Pileser, also known as Pul (see 2 Kings 16:7-8). Pul received the lavish gift and soundly defeated Damascus carrying them away (2 Kings 16:9). However, this was already likely in his plans and he provided no real security for Ahaz. In fact, he brought further distress when other nations, like Edom and Philistia, rose up against Judah (2 Chronicles 28:16-21).

A fitting epitaph of my father's life is written in the Bible. Fill in the blanks by selecting the correct words from this list: *Ahaz, moral, Judah, LORD, unfaithful*. For help, see 2 Chronicles 28:19.

Fill in the blanks

"For the _____ brought _____ low because of _____ king of Israel, for he had encouraged _____ decline in Judah and had been continually _____ to the LORD."

I became king during the third year of Hoshea, the last king of Israel. My name is Hezekiah and my name means "strength of Jehovah." Due to Ahaz, Judah was weakened, but God strengthened me in the challenges my administration faced. His prophets, Isaiah, Micah, and Hosea proved true. Will Judah survive the violent invasion of Assyria? My name is Hezekiah. *Come walk with me in my history!*

True or false

1. **T or F** A child can turn away from his father's example to do good or evil.
2. **T or F** Ahaz was wicked like the kings of Israel.
3. **T or F** Ahaz behaved wickedly because his father, Jotham was wicked.
4. **T or F** Hezekiah ruled more like his ancient ancestor David, rather than his father Ahaz.

LESSON 10 Walking With King Hezekiah: Strengthened by God

5. **T or F** Isaiah prophesied during the days of Hezekiah.

6. **T or F** Assyria was the major political threat to Israel and Judah at this time.

The Lord strengthened Hezekiah to restore Scriptural worship in Judah (2 Chronicles 29-30)

While Israel had nineteen kings, Hezekiah was only the twelfth king of Judah.[1] His first priority was to restore true worship which he began in his first year and the first month of his reign (2 Chronicles 29:3).

- *This involved cleaning the house and repairing the house of God (2 Chronicles 29:4-19).* Where Hezekiah's father cast these holy things aside, Hezekiah had them restored (2 Chronicles 29:19).

- *This involved implementing temple worship (2 Chronicles 29:20-36).* Hezekiah demonstrated faithful zeal rising early in the morning to gather the rulers of the city to make atonement. They brought seven bulls, seven rams, seven lambs, and seven male goats for a sin offering for all Israel (2 Chronicles 29:20-24). Then the Levites added music with the burnt offering. This praise followed the commandments of the prophets for Israel (2 Chronicles 29:25-30). We do not have Levites, animal sacrifices, or an earthly priesthood in the church today. When some wrongly want to add the instruments of David to worship, they do not try to add the sacrifices David nor the Levitical priesthood. Old Testament saints were commanded to offer sacrifices, have a special priesthood, and play various stringed instruments and trumpets (2 Chronicles 29:25). However, Jesus died to

> In the first year of his reign, in the first month, he **opened** the doors of the **house of the Lord** and **repaired** them.
>
> - 2 Chronicles 29:3

---

[1] This count of Israel's kings excludes a man called Tibni. Although half the people of Israel wanted to "make" Tibni king, it seems evident that he never became one as the people who followed Omri prevailed and Tibni was put to death (1 Kings 16:20-21).

bring in the New Testament and we must follow it if we are going to please God. Jesus has commanded us through the apostles to offer music from the heart, not a mechanical harp (Ephesians 5:19; Hebrews 13:15).

- *This involved celebrating the Passover (2 Chronicles 30).* They could not celebrate the Passover at its regular time because there was an insufficient number of priests and the people had not gathered to Jerusalem. They agreed to celebrate the Passover in the second month according to what Moses permitted in Numbers 9:1-14. Hezekiah reached out to get people to obey the Lord. They sent runners who carried letters from the king and his leaders pleading with them to obey the Lord and come to the feast. They went even as far as Dan inviting people to Jerusalem to offer God true worship. The people in Israel generally rejected the invitation and mocked these messengers but there were some from the tribes who humbled themselves and traveled to Jerusalem (2 Chronicles 30:11). The people of Judah were unified to obey the king and the Lord (2 Chronicles 30:12). The Feast was a great success and was filled with gladness and singing (2 Chronicles 30:21). It was also a time of teaching, confession, and prayer (2 Chronicles 30:22, 27).

Questions

7. Why did the Levites use mechanical instruments in their worship?
   _____
   _____

8. From Ephesians 5:19, name some characteristics of New Testament music. _____
   _____

9. Runners carried the king's letters inviting all Israel to come and participate in true worship.

    a. Who is our King? _____

    b. What letters did He give us? _____
       _____
       _____

    c. Who should we invite today (see Matthew 28:18-20)? _____
       _____
       _____

LESSON 10 Walking With King Hezekiah: Strengthened by God 79

    d. What does true worship look like today? See John 4:23-24; 8:31; Acts 2:42; Colossians 3:16-17._____

_____

_____

_____

The Lord strengthened Hezekiah to remove false religion from the land (2 Chronicles 31:1)

Read 2 Kings 18:4-7. Hezekiah knew that the only Scriptural place for altar worship was Jerusalem. He actively taught and defended this truth. His enemies referenced this doctrine.

Fill in the blanks

2 Chronicles 32:12
"Has not the same Hezekiah taken away His _____ places and His _____, and commanded Judah and Jerusalem, saying, 'You shall worship before _____ _____ and burn incense on it'?"

Hezekiah was not only for the right worship, but he also opposed wrong worship. Knowing there is one altar means all the other altars are false and unauthorized; therefore, he removed the high places. In his faithful zeal for Jehovah, he also broke the bronze serpent. Long before Israel was in the Promised Land, Moses had fashioned a bronze serpent for people to look at so that they could be healed from deadly snake bites (Numbers 21:5-9). This image was never intended to become an object of worship. Although it was once used as a condition through which people could be saved, and although it was an ancient relic built by Moses, it had become an instrument for idolatry. Hezekiah broke it in pieces and called it Nehushtan, which means "a piece of brass."

Questions

10. What about people who wear replicas of a man put on cross? How are we to remember the crucified savior? Read 1 Corinthians 11:24-25.

_____

_____

_____

11. What about others who pray through images of a man on a cross today? Is this idolatry also? _____

_____

_____

"Be **strong** and **courageous**; do not be **afraid** nor **dismayed** before the king of Assyria, nor before all the multitude that is with him; for there are **more** with us than with him. With him is an arm of **flesh**; but with us is the **LORD our God**, to help us and to **fight** our battles." And the people were **strengthened** by the words of Hezekiah king of Judah.

- 2 Chronicles 32:7-8

The Lord strengthened Hezekiah to restore support for the Levites (2 Chronicles 31:2-4)

The people were commanded to give tithes (a tenth) of their provisions to the priests so that the priests could devote themselves to the Law of the Lord. The people fully obeyed and gave so much that heaps of offerings formed. When the leaders saw such, they blessed the Lord and His people (2 Chronicles 31:8). Hezekiah ordered that storerooms should be built to hold these offerings.

The Lord strengthened Hezekiah to face the threats of an ungodly emperor (2 Chronicles 32:1-23)

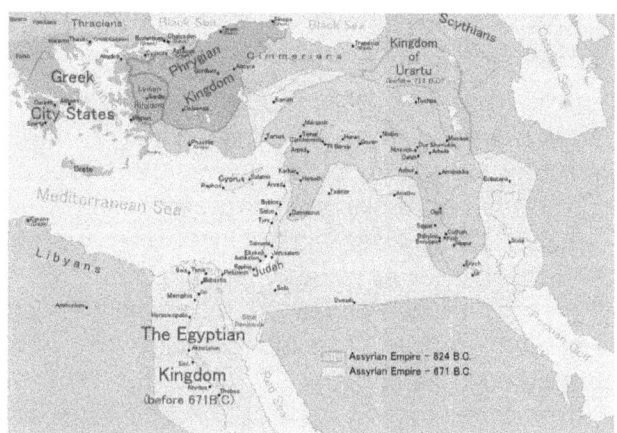

Assyria's empire is expanding and overwhelms Israel in 722 BC. In the same year, the Assyrian king, Shalmaneser V died. His brother, Sargon II, took the throne away and completed the siege against Samaria, the capital city. Sargon died in a campaign in 705 BC. His son, Sennacherib, became king and turned his attention toward Hezekiah to conquer Judah. In Hezekiah's fourteenth year he was scared into submission and paid what was imposed (2 Kings 18:13-16). However, he was later encouraged by Isaiah and did not shrink away from rebelling against Assyria. Hezekiah made preparations.

LESSON 10 Walking With King Hezekiah: Strengthened by God

First, he redirected the Gihon springs so that Jerusalem would not perish with thirst during the siege (2 Chronicles 32:1-4, 30). The 1,750-foot tunnel that Hezekiah had men dig to redirect this spring has been discovered.

Second, he also repaired the wall and built another wall outside (2 Chronicles 32:5). Archaeology has also discovered remnants of this wall. Third, he prepared weapons and shields so that his soldiers could better defend the city. Fourth, he prayed and the Lord answered his prayer (2 Kings 19:20).

Sennacherib sent messengers to blaspheme Jehovah and belittle Hezekiah to try to break their faith. Yet they kept their trust in God. Sennacherib's messenger, the Rabshakeh[3],

Hezekiahs Tunnel
Daniel Wong from Newark, CA, USA[2]

warned the people to not listen to Hezekiah nor trust in Jehovah (2 Kings 18:28-30). Letters reviling the Lord God were written comparing Jehovah to other gods that had fallen before Assyrian domination (2 Chronicles 32:17). When Hezekiah and Isaiah prayed out to the Lord, He delivered them by sending an angel against the Assyrian camp who killed 185,000 soldiers (2 Chronicles 32:20-21). Sennacherib returned in shame and was at some point assassinated by his own son while in the temple of his god. This fulfilled what Isaiah prophesied (Isaiah 37:6-8). His inflated version of his conquest against Hezekiah has been preserved where he boasted how he took 46 strong-walled cities of Judah in what is called the Taylor Prism.

Taylor Prism
David Castor, public domain image

He slightly recognized his failure against Hezekiah even in his own words. He claimed that he shut Hezekiah "up in Jerusalem, his royal city, like a bird in a cage." While he did surround and shut Hezekiah up like a bird in a cage, he never took over the cage! Unlike Samaria, Sennacherib failed the conquest against Judah by failing to take the royal city. The Bible tells us why. The battle belongs to the Lord!

---

[2] https://commons.wikimedia.org/wiki/File:Hezekiahs_Tunnel.jpg, https://creativecommons.org/licenses/by-sa/2.0/legalcode
[3] It has been discovered that this ancient and lost term refers to one like a chief of staff. The use of this word and others by the author of 2 Kings and by Isaiah (Isaiah 36:2; 2 Kings 18:17; etc.) gives support that the writers were eyewitnesses of these events.

Questions

12. What did Hezekiah do with the bronze serpent that Moses had made? Why? _____
_____
_____

13. How many warriors of Assyria did the angel of the Lord kill (see 2 Kings 19:35)?_____

14. Why was it important to Hezekiah for the priests and Levites to be supported? _____
_____
_____

15. Which Assyrian king came up against Samaria and besieged it (2 Kings 18:9)? _____

16. How many years did it take to conquer Samaria, the capital of Israel (2 Kings 18:10)?_____

17. Why did the city of Samaria fall (2 Kings 18:11-12)? _____
_____
_____

18. Why did the city of Jerusalem not fall? _____
_____
_____

19. What did Hezekiah do to prepare for Sennacherib's invasion? _____
_____
_____

20. How important is prayer? Do you pray to God about your fears? Do you thank God in prayer when He delivers you from what you fear?_____
_____
_____

21. Can you name any songs that we sing that teach us how God is our strength or that we ought to always trust in the Lord for deliverance?
_____
_____
_____

Walking Into the Collapse and Fall of a Kingdom

Lesson 11

Israel's collapse

Israel and Judah were doomed to destruction. Israel's capital city, Samaria, fell in 722 BC, being overtaken by Assyrian forces who forced their departure from the land. Israel was plagued with political instability. Kings were assassinated four different times within a span of about 30 years! The Assyrian empire had become very strong and conquered the land from the Persian Gulf down to Egypt. To make matters worse, Israel hastened its destruction by pursuing the things the Lord hated. The Lord's warnings continually fell on deaf ears resulting in their destruction.

Among the last kings of Israel were Jehu then Jehoahaz his son. The military suffered during Jehoahaz's rule (2 Kings 13:7). His son Joash became king after him. He is also referred to as Jehoash. Elisha died during Joash's reign (2 Kings 13:14-20). Jeroboam, Joash's son ascended the throne. He is often referred to as Jeroboam II. Jonah the prophet had spoken of this king's resurgence of territorial recovery (2 Kings 14:25). Amos and Hosea were also prophets during this time. Where Jeroboam II reigned 41 years, his son, Zechariah had the throne for only six months (2 Kings 14:23; 15:8). He was assassinated by Shallum (2 Kings 15:8-13). Yet Shallum was assassinated a month later by Menahem. After Menahem's rule, his son, Pekahiah began to rule but he was assassinated by his officer, Pekah!

During Pekah's rule, the powerful Assyrian king, Tiglath-Pileser, took several of his cities and carried away many Israelites (2 Kings 15:27-29). Hoshea, the son of Elah led a conspiracy and assassinated Pekah. Hoshea was the last king of Israel when Samaria fell. Not only were the Israelites carried

KEY PASSAGE

Yet the **LORD** testified against **Israel** and against **Judah**, by all of His prophets, every seer, saying, "**Turn** from your **evil ways**, and keep My **commandments** and My statutes, according to all the **law** which I commanded your **fathers**, and which I sent to you by My servants the **prophets**." Nevertheless they **would not hear**, but stiffened their necks, like the necks of their fathers, who did **not believe** in the LORD their God.

- 2 Kings 17:13-14

away and placed into foreign lands, but foreigners replaced them in Samaria. These became the ancestors of the Samaritans we read of in the New Testament.

Questions

1. What year did Samaria fall and who conquered the city? _____
   _____

2. Name the four sons of Jehu who reigned as king. _____
   _____
   _____

3. Read 2 Kings 17:13-18 and answer the following questions.

   a. Did God give Israel any warning about their sins? _____

   b. What did they do with the warning?_____
   _____

   c. Who influenced Israel and Judah to sin? _____
   _____

   d. Why did God remove Israel out of His sight? _____
   _____

   e. In a similar way, what will God do with sinners who refuse to repent and obey the gospel in the final judgment? See 2 Thessalonians 1:9.
   _____
   _____

Judah's collapse

The kingdom of Judah endured longer than the kingdom of Israel. Judah survived and retained its independence from the Assyrian rule but would later be conquered by Nebuchadnezzar, king of Babylon. Judah's judgment was delayed because there were times in which they repented and sought the Lord. However, they grew worse and worse over time. After King Hezekiah died. His son, Manasseh reigned for 55 years. Everything that was right about Hezekiah was missing in Manasseh. Hezekiah called the people back to the Lord. However "Manasseh seduced them to do more evil than the nations whom the LORD had destroyed before the children of Israel" (2 Kings 21:9). Manasseh became the Ahab of Judah.

Fill in the blanks

LESSON 11 Walking Into the Collapse and Fall of a Kingdom

2 Kings 21:3
"For he _____ the high places which _____ his _____ had destroyed; he raised up altars for _____, and made a wooden image, as _____ king of Israel had done; and he worshiped all the host of heaven and served them."

He rebuilt the high places Hezekiah had destroyed. He worshipped Baal and Asherah, Canaanite gods. He sacrificed his sons in the fire. He also practiced black arts by using witchcraft. In addition, he shed innocent blood (2 Kings 21:16). He behaved with greater wickedness than even the Amorites who once populated this area (2 Kings 21:11). In his days, God pronounced the death sentence against Judah.

Notice the three "I will's" of 2 Kings 21:13-14.

- *I will stretch over Jerusalem the measuring line.* This is called the measuring line of Samaria. God's standard of righteousness did not change from Israel to Judah. He would punish Judah for the same crimes that Israel was punished for.

- *I will wipe Jerusalem.* God describes Jerusalem's overthrow as a man who takes a bowl then wipes away the food from the inside and turns it upside down. The word translated "wipe" is the same Hebrew word that God used when speaking of the world's destruction in the days of Noah, in which He wiped out all living things on the face of the earth through the floodwaters (Genesis 7:4).

- *I will forsake.* The penalty of unforsaken sin is to become forsaken by God. God gave them up to calamity even as He gave up Gentiles who suppressed the truth of God to live dishonorable lives (Romans 1:24). Psalm 81:12 reads, "So I gave them over to their own stubborn heart, To walk in their own counsels." Any relationship with God is based on conditions from God. David warned Solomon that if he forsook the Lord, God would cast him off forever (1 Chronicles 28:9).

Questions

4. From 2 Kings 21:3–9, list all the sins of Manasseh. _____
_____
_____
_____

5. What did God promise to do to Judah? _____
_____

6. Look up the verses below and identify the penalties of sin.

> He **burned** the house of the **LORD** and the **king's** house; all the houses of **Jerusalem**, that is, all the houses of the **great**, he burned with **fire**. And all the **army** of the Chaldeans who were with the captain of the guard **broke down** the **walls** of Jerusalem all around.
>
> - 2 Kings 25:9-10

a. Genesis 2:16-17 _____

b. Proverbs 11:19 _____

c. Romans 6:23 _____

d. Isaiah 59:2 _____

Judah's captivity

After Manasseh died, his son Amon became king and only reigned for two years. He was wicked and met an untimely death being assassinated in his own house by his servants. However, the people of the land executed the killers and made his son Josiah king at the age of eight. Josiah was an exceptional king. He rejected the wickedness of his father and served the Lord with a loyal heart. The Book of the Law had been lost (likely during Manasseh's reign). It was found in Josiah's day. Upon the reading of it, Josiah tore his clothes fearing God's wrath. He humbled himself and wept before the Lord. God heard his prayer and gave him peace. Josiah understood that God expects nothing short of our all. He was genuinely committed to following the Lord with his all.

Fill in the blanks

2 Kings 23:25
"Now before him there was no king like him, who _____ to the LORD with all his _____, with all his _____, and with all his _____, according to all the Law of Moses; nor after him did any arise like him."

Josiah's godliness did not turn the Lord's wrath away from Judah (2 Kings 23:26-27). Doom was only temporarily delayed. It is likely that the majority of the people of Judah were corrupt and living godless lives (Jeremiah 5:11).

LESSON 11 Walking Into the Collapse and Fall of a Kingdom   87

The Assyrian rule was diminishing, and Babylonian power was on the rise. Nabopolassar had already rebelled against Assyria and became king of Babylon in 626 BC. The rapidly declining Assyrian empire met its end in 609 BC at the Battle of Harran. In this year Pharaoh Necho went to assist Assyria against Babylon. Josiah and the army of Judah opposed Pharaoh's march but to the dismay of many, Josiah was fatally struck by an archer. His final words in Scripture are, "Take me away, for I am severely wounded" (2 Chronicles 35:23). Jeremiah, a prophet during his time and author of the book of Jeremiah and Lamentations mourned over his death with many others (2 Chronicles 35:24-25). The last great king in Judah was dead.

His son, Jehoahaz became king and only reigned for three months. Jehoahaz used his little time to do evil. Pharaoh carried him off to Egypt where he died in prison.

Pharaoh made his brother Eliakim king and changed his name to Jehoiakim. Jehoiakim was a very wicked king who resisted the words of the prophets and shed innocent blood (cf. Jeremiah 26:20-23). He was everything his father Josiah was not. Rather than trembling at the word of God, Jehoiakim was unteachable. On one occasion, he interrupted the reading of the scroll written by Jeremiah, cut it up and cast it into the hearth (Jeremiah 36:23). Yet the word of God remains. Jeremiah wrote another scroll with these words and added similar words to its content (Jeremiah 36:32). Jehoiakim would be punished with death and without lamentations. His death would be treated like that of a donkey that dies (Jeremiah 22:18-19).

First deportation (605 BC)

Nebuchadnezzar succeeded his father, Nabopolassar, as king of Babylon in 605 BC. That same year Nebuchadnezzar defeated Egypt in the Battle of Carchemish and pursued them to their own land. This was also the year Jeremiah made the seventy-year-captivity prophecy (Jeremiah 25:1-11).

In 605 BC, Nebuchadnezzar also invaded Judah. There were three separate deportations that affected Judah. Daniel and his three friends were of the very first Jews taken away to Babylon in 605 (Daniel 1:1-2).

Second deportation (597 BC)

Jehoiakim became Nebuchadnezzar's vassal king but when he rebelled, Nebuchadnezzar made a return trip to Palestine in 598 BC. Jehoiakim had previously died before Nebuchadnezzar returned and his son, Jehoiachin (also named Jeconiah and Coniah) became king. He only reigned three months when Nebuchadnezzar carried him away with the articles of gold and about ten thousand others in 597 BC leaving only the poorest in the land (2 Kings 24:13-16). The prophet Ezekiel was also taken away at this time (Ezekiel 1:1-3).

Third deportation (587 BC)

Nebuchadnezzar made Mattaniah, (Jechoniah's uncle) king and changed his name to Zedekiah. Zedekiah was the last king of Judah and reigned eleven years (2 Kings 24:18). He eventually rebelled against Nebuchadnezzar also. As punishment, his sons were executed before him and then his eyes were put out and he was carried away to Babylon in 587 BC. In that year the temple of the Lord was burned, the walls were broken, the city was destroyed, and the rest of the people were expelled from the land. The kingdom of Judah had come to an end according to the word of the Lord.

True or false

7. **T or F** Josiah was the last godly king reigning in Judah.
8. **T or F** Nebuchadnezzar ascended his father's throne in 605 BC.
9. **T or F** Daniel was carried away in the first deportation in 605 BC.
10. **T or F** Ezekiel was carried away in the third deportation in 587 BC.
11. **T or F** Ten thousand Jews were carried into Babylonian captivity in 597 BC.
12. **T or F** Jeremiah prophesied of an eighty-year captivity period.
13. **T or F** The Egyptian military overpowered the Babylonians at Carchemish in 605 BC.
14. **T or F** Nebuchadnezzar destroyed Solomon's temple in 587 BC.

Questions

15. Define "deportation." _____
   _____
   _____

16. This is the lowest part of Israel's history. What was the cause of this fall and what are some things Judah lost? _____
   _____
   _____

17. When Jehoiakim cut up and burned Jeremiah's scroll, did that change what God's word said or what God would do? _____

LESSON 11 Walking Into the Collapse and Fall of a Kingdom 89

18. How might people treat the Bible with contempt today? _____
_____
_____
_____
_____

Conclusion

This is the second most important part of Israelite history. The temple was destroyed; spiritually, they are lost. The throne is destroyed; politically, they are no longer a nation. Their land is desolated; they are disinherited from the promises made to Abraham. Carried away as captives, they're brought back to where they began—being a people under bondage. This time period demonstrates the destructive nature of sin.

Lesson 12

Walking With Ezra to Rebuild the Law in Israel

"By the rivers of Babylon, there we sat down, yea, we wept when we remembered Zion. We hung our harps upon the willows in the midst of it. For there those who carried us away captive asked of us a song, and those who plundered us requested mirth, saying, 'Sing us one of the songs of Zion!' How shall we sing the LORD'S song In a foreign land?" (Psalm 137:1-4).

After the second deportation of the Jews in 597 BC, Jeremiah wrote a letter to the captives and told them to resume as much of a normal life as could be found by building houses, planting gardens, taking wives and having children. He told our people to seek peace. He also warned against the false prophets who would deceive them with false messages of a premature release and return. This captivity was real and so was its specified time of seventy years. These and other teachings are found in Jeremiah 29.

The return of the exiles began with a proclamation of Cyrus, king of Persia in 539 BC and centered upon the rebuilding of the temple of the Lord. Cyrus even put it in writing that our people were to return to our homeland and reconstruct a new temple unto the Lord (Ezra 1:1-4).

Cyrus also returned the articles of gold and silver that Nebuchadnezzar had taken out of Solomon's temple. These totaled five thousand four hundred articles. These articles were placed under the authority of the prince of Judah, Sheshbazzar (Ezra 1:5-11). Sheshbazzar's Hebrew name is Zerubbabel which means sown in Babylon. He is a descendant of the great king David, being the grandson of King Jeconiah (Matthew 1:12).

> **KEY PASSAGE**
>
> For Ezra had **prepared** his **heart** to seek the **Law** of the LORD, and to **do** it, and to teach **statutes** and **ordinances** in Israel.
>
> - Ezra 7:10

Through discouraging times, the temple was finally rebuilt in the sixth year of Darius the Great (Ezra 6:15). Those who were old enough to see Solomon's temple thought the glory of this temple was inferior and they wept over it (Ezra 3:12; Haggai 2:3). Yet Haggai prophesied that the glory of this temple will be greater than Solomon's and that God would give peace in this place (Haggai 2:8). This hope-filled prophecy would likely be connected with the Messiah who would come and grace the temple with His presence (Malachi 3:1). When the temple was rebuilt, a great step was accomplished! Worship was restored to Jehovah. This shows a spiritual restoration with God.

Many years after the temple's completion, I will lead a second group of captives to Jerusalem with the focus on rebuilding the law. Subsequent to this, Nehemiah will lead an effort to rebuild the broken walls around Jerusalem. I am a scribe, devoting my life to living and teaching the precepts of God. My name is Ezra. *Come walk with me in my history!*

Fill in the blanks

Ezra 7:10
"For Ezra had _____ his _____ to seek the _____ of the _____, and to _____ it, and to _____ statutes and ordinances in Israel."

Questions

1. How large was the company of Jews who returned to Judah (Ezra 2:64)?
   _____

2. How many servants were there (Ezra 2:65)?_____

3. How many singers? _____

4. What do the restoration of worship and the rebuilding of the temple signify? _____
   _____

5. Before we teach others, what must we first do?_____
   _____

After the events of Queen Esther and during the reign of Artaxerxes in 457 BC, Ezra entered Jerusalem in the fifth month of his seventh year. Ezra found favor in the sight of King Artaxerxes and wrote him a letter encouraging him to beautify the house of God, teach the Law of God, appoint magistrates and judges and to impose judgments of lawbreakers with the appropriate penalty (Ezra 7).

LESSON 12 Walking With Ezra to Rebuild the Law in Israel

The problem of wrong marriages (Ezra 9)

One of the chief problems in Ezra's day was that the people had intermarried with peoples of the land, violating the Law of Moses (Deuteronomy 7:3-4). Many priests also participated in this error. Some of these marriages even had resulted in children. What was Ezra to do? The first thing he did was tear his clothes and sit down, being astonished at what he had learned. He sat fasting until the evening sacrifice. The sins of his people deeply affected this scribe. Ezra was not indifferent regarding sin but felt overwhelmed by it, knowing how God views it. The second thing he did was go to his God in a prayer filled with deep humility, sorrow, and requests for mercy.

The solution to wrong marriages (Ezra 10)

For a saint that has fallen into sin, the solution given in Scripture is constant. Regardless of the sin, the solution to committing a trespass remains the same regardless of how emotional the situation becomes. The emotions of the situation do not define the solution; rather, the word of God does. What must be done?

First, the sinner must recognize that he has violated God's law (Ezra 10:1). While Ezra was weeping over the sin, a large gathering occurred where the people also began weeping bitterly over their sins. Until a person recognizes his sin and feels guilt over it, he will never correct it.

Fill in the blanks

Ezra 7:10-11

"Then Ezra the priest stood up and said to them, 'You have _____ and have taken pagan wives, adding to the guilt of Israel. Now therefore, make _____ to the _____ _____ of your fathers, and do His will; _____ yourselves from the peoples of the land, and from the _____ _____.'"

> If we **confess** our **sins**, He is faithful and just to **forgive** us our sins and to **cleanse** us from all unrighteousness. If we say that we have **not sinned**, we make Him a **liar**, and His **word** is not in us.
>
> - 1 John 1:9-10

Second, the sinner needs to confess his sin to God (Ezra 10:2). He must come to the full understanding that he has violated God's law and confess that to his God. It is not a pretend law or even the law of man that he has broken, rather, it is the law of the Ruler of the Universe. He must see that and go to Him for forgiveness.

Mercy and spiritual health are given to one who confesses his crime to his God. King David wrote in Psalm 41:4, "I said, 'LORD, be merciful to me; Heal my soul, for I have sinned against You.'"

Third, the sinner needs to put away the sin. In this case, the sinners needed to put away their pagan wives and their children (Ezra 10:19, 44). There will be those who oppose doing the right thing even as Jonathan and Jahaziah did in Ezra 10:15. But to please the Lord, the sinner must separate himself from the relationship and action that is sinful.

Thought questions

Jesus taught that a man and woman were to remain married until death separates them (Matthew 19:3-9). Jesus gave only one reason where a man could put away his wife and remarry and that was for sexual immorality.

1. What should a man do who wants to please God but had in the past put his wife away for some other reason and remarried a second person? _____
   _____

2. Would the solution to that sin change if he had children with his second wife? _____

3. Will everyone accept the Lord's teaching (see Matthew 19:10-12)? _____

4. Ezra was a tremendous leader of God's people. Look up the passages below and list a quality of Ezra that enabled him to be such a great leader.
   Ezra 7:6 _____
   Ezra 7:10 _____
   Ezra 8:21 _____
   Ezra 8:22 _____
   Ezra 10:1 _____
   Ezra 10:6 _____

Conclusion

Ezra provides us a good example of how a leader of God's people should be. He was touched by the sins of his brethren and worked to have these sins corrected in a compassionate yet bold way. His work was important to restoring the law unto God's people. Without this, the Jews could not progress. Their strength was conditioned upon their faithfulness to God. We should always revere God's word and carefully follow it with the dedication Ezra had.

Walking With Nehemiah to Rebuild the Walls of Jerusalem

Lesson 13

I am Nehemiah, the son of Hachaliah. I serve as a cupbearer to Artaxerxes, the great king of Persia. In 446 BC I received word about the people of God in Judah. The walls of Jerusalem lie in ruin. The gates were burned and the walls were broken down by the Babylonians and had never since been rebuilt. Hearing of the distress my brethren were in and the condition of the holy city of Jerusalem troubled me.

I determined to go back to Judah but I needed permission from the king. One day he noticed that I was sad which frightened me (Nehemiah 2:2). Someone who serves before the monarch must be content so long as he fares well. Looking sad could be wrongly interpreted and cause suspicion on his part. I quickly prayed to God and then proceded to tell the king what was in my heart regarding my home city. He granted me to take leave of my duties and return to Jerusalem providing me letters that permitted me to travel through the regions patrolled by various governors. Additionally, he provided me a letter to Asaph, the keeper of the kings' forest, to provide me timber. He also sent an army escort with me.

My arrival instantly made some enemies with those who despise our nation. Sanballat the Horonite, Tobiah the Ammonite, and Geshem the Arab were dangerously powerful adversaries to me and my work. What obstacles will I face? What will be involved in such a reconstructive effort as this? Can this project be accomplished in the face of such enemies? My name is Nehemiah. *Come walk with me in my history!*

KEY PASSAGE

So the **wall** was **finished** on the twenty-fifth day of Elul, in fifty-two days. And it happened, when all our **enemies** heard of it, and all the **nations** around us saw these things, that they were very **disheartened** in their own eyes; for they **perceived** that this **work** was done by our **God**.

- Nehemiah 6:15-16

Facing the facts (Nehemiah 2:11-16)

Before any great project can be accomplished, a sober assessment of the facts, the obstacles, the demands, the cost, the calculation of time and effort should be made. After being in Jerusalem for three days, Nehemiah scouted about the ruins of the wall in the night. That it was night shows he privately wanted to evaluate the damage without friend or foe knowing.

Cooperation (Nehemiah 2:17-18)

The hand of God was there to enable Nehemiah in this work. But often, God's hand requires our hands to be involved. Projects can look too large for one person, but many hands make light work. When each person does something, great things happen. Nehemiah knew that he needed the cooperation of many minds and the strength of many arms to complete this reconstruction process.

Fill in the blanks

Nehemiah 2:18
"And I told them of the _____ of my _____ which had been good upon me, and also of the king's words that he had spoken to me. So they said, 'Let _____ rise _____ and _____.' Then they set their _____ to this _____ _____."

Chapter three bears out that members from all classes were expected to carry their share of the load.

The seven tactics of the opposition

Building the wall was good for the Jews, and their enemies knew it (Nehemiah 2:18). The enemies of God's people will use different tactics to destroy good work. Some of these are found in the opposition to building the walls.

- *Anger (Nehemiah 1:1)*
  This is similar to what many Jewish leaders were guilty of in the New Testament. They commanded the apostles to not preach in the name of Jesus and when the apostles continued, they were furious (Acts 5:33).

- *Ridicule and contempt (Nehemiah 4:1-3)*
  To mock and make fun of something good is to show contempt for that work. The purpose is to try to convince others and the workers to reconsider the value of what they are doing to slow the project or stop it altogether.

LESSON 13 Walking With Nehemiah to Rebuild the Walls of Jerusalem

Nehemiah gives us two answers when facing ridicule from unbelievers (Nehemiah 4:4-6). First, he went to God in prayer and laid his adversaries' sins before the Lord. It is important to note that Nehemiah did not flag these crimes for personal crimes, but rather, they were attacks against God "for they have provoked You to anger before the builders" (4:5). Second, Nehemiah and the people opted to do the very opposite reaction that the opposition wanted. In this case, they went to work (4:6). This work continued on; the ridicule was left for God to judge. The people put their mental and physical energy into the work. For the church's work to move forward, we must also have a mind to work and not become distracted by the world's insults.

- *Conspiracy and confusing (Nehemiah 4:7-8)*
A powerful tool Satan uses against good works is to sow seeds of fear and confusion into the hearts of the workers. After Saul was converted to Jesus in the New Testament he confounded the Jews in Damascus proving that Jesus was the Christ. Rather than repenting and being converted to Jesus, they plotted or conspired to put Paul to death (Acts 9:22-23). Some would rather kill the messenger than kill their wrong beliefs.

Questions

1. Name two things Nehemiah did to deal with his enemies' conspiracy to cause confusion. See Nehemiah 4:9. _____
   _____
   _____
   _____

- *Discouragement (Nehemiah 4:10-12)*
Discouragement can become one of Satan's most effective tools to stop good works.

> Nevertheless we made our **prayer** to our **God**, and because of them we set a **watch** against them **day and night**.
>
> - Nehemiah 4:9

Discouragement is an internal foe that settles into the heart and can become a cause of complaints. While traveling to the Promised Land, Israel became discouraged and grumbled against Moses and the Lord (Numbers 21:4-5). In addition to external threats and conspiracies, there stood seemingly insurmountable heaps of rubbish that prohibited future building. Much clearing away needed to be done before any building could be done. The effect was that the strength of the workers began to decay. The progress was slowed and the obstacles became overly large. Such can be the case when one is exhausted.

However, the heart of man gains much resolve when it is refreshed with purpose. Nehemiah did a couple of things to destroy discouragement. He positioned men at the weakest parts of the wall as a guard. He also set the people to work according to their families. Nothing can be better organized or strong than a family unit that works together. It reminds us of who we are and our purpose. These families may have been stationed near their very residences. Nehemiah reminded them to remember the Lord and fight for their families and houses (Nehemiah 4:14). Nehemiah had half the company work in construction while the other half carried weapons for battle (Nehemiah 4:16-17).

Nehemiah also set up an alarm system because these groups were separated from others by some distance. If a potential danger appeared, they were to sound the trumpet and all were to rally at that point to fight. All in all, gaining courage is the best medicine for being discouraged. Knowing that your brethren are going through the same struggles can have a positive effect on our thinking.

- *Craftiness (Nehemiah 6:1-4)*
  Sanballat and his allies sent a letter to Nehemiah four times to get him to leave his work to come to meet with them. It was likely that they wanted to get Nehemiah away from his work so that they could murder him. There are some people whose actions have been so evil that they are not worthy to meet and have discussions.

- *Intimidation and slander (Nehemiah 6:5-9)*
  Satan has often used intimidation to get good people to stop doing God's work. Sanballat next tried to blackmail Nehemiah with a slanderous message. He redefined the events that were going on in Jerusalem to look like Nehemiah had the ambition to become a king to rebel against Persian rule. He threatened to send this letter to the king if Nehemiah did not meet with him. He denied the false allegation and made prayer to God for strength.

LESSON 13 Walking With Nehemiah to Rebuild the Walls of Jerusalem

- *Compromise (Nehemiah 6:10-13)*
  Shemaiah was the son of Delaiah, likely a well-known person of that time who evidently was the head of a priestly house (see 1 Chronicles 24:18). His son Shemaiah likely carried some influence, as he was able to get Nehemiah to come to his house. However, he was a traitor (even as Judas betrayed Jesus) and was a secret informer to Tobiah and Sanballat. His conversation with Nehemiah was to make him afraid in order to get him to compromise the law, breaking something that was explicitly forbidden. He wanted Nehemiah to go into the sanctuary and shut the doors to save his life from some perceived threat to his life.

  How could Nehemiah know that Shemaiah was a false teacher? He didn't judge his message based on how pious his father was, but rather on the content of what was spoken. First, the governor should not flee. What kind of message would this send to the people? Second, Shemaiah was wanting Nehemiah to do something that the Law would have judged as being worthy of death. Only those descendants of Aaron serving as priests were permitted to enter this place. The outsider was to be put to death (Numbers 18:7). Judah's history showed the folly of a king who tried entering the holy place to offer incense (2 Chronicles 26:18-21). Knowing this example with King Uzziah and that God's commandments do not change, Nehemiah was able to discern that Shemaiah was a false prophet. We cannot do evil that good may come (Romans 3:8).

Fill in the blanks

Nehemiah 6:12
"Then I _____ that God had _____ _____ him at all, but that he _____ this _____ against me because Tobiah and Sanballat had _____ him."

Thought questions

2. The enemies of Nehemiah said and did a lot of things against God's people and God's work. What did the enemies of John and Jesus say about them (see Luke 7:33-34)? _____
   _____

3. Can you think of ways that God's people are ridiculed today? What will you do if you are made fun of for promoting the truth that is found in Jesus? _____
   _____
   _____
   _____

4. How many times did Nehemiah's enemies ask him to come and meet? What was Nehemiah's answer (Nehemiah 6:3-4)? Did Nehemiah need to change his answer based on the growing number of times he was asked? _____
   _____
   _____

5. Nehemiah could draw from the written Law of God to safeguard from being deceived. How can we know if someone is a false teacher today and what should our duty be as listeners (1 John 4:1-2 Peter 2:1-2; Acts 17:11)? _____
   _____
   _____

Conclusion

Through Nehemiah's leadership, the walls were completed in only 52 days. By continuing this work and completing it, the enemies were disheartened and perceived that this work was from God (Nehemiah 6:16). Likewise, only when we fully submit to God and resist the devil will he flee from us (James 4:7). He will move to look for easier prey.

Despite facing many obstacles, Nehemiah accomplished this feat by demonstrating great leadership qualities. He drew from God's inspired word, prayer, wisdom for problem-solving, and sheer courage that came through faith-building. He faced other obstacles after the walls were built, but the same recipe for success is what he used.

As you go through your life in these early years, build your faith on the One who changes not so that you will have the needed wisdom and courage to face the many obstacles to come. Keep these words in your heart: "Remember the Lord, great and awesome, and fight for your brethren" (Nehemiah 4:14).

www.ingramcontent.com/pod-product-compliance
Lightning Source LLC
Chambersburg PA
CBHW070622050426
42450CB00011B/3108